The Unholy Ghost Murder
A True Crime Tale, Texas-Style

© 2012 J.B. Smith

Manufactured in the United States.

For information, please contact:
www.sheriffjbsmith.com

ISBN: 9781479206216

THE UNHOLY GHOST MURDER

A True Crime Tale, Texas-Style

Sheriff J.B. Smith
with
Roy Maynard

Texas Sheriff J.B. Smith, one of the state's longest-serving sheriffs, was continually elected from 1976 until his retirement in 2012. He earned an associate's degree from Tyler Junior College and his bachelor of science degree in criminal justice from the University of Texas at Tyler. He's a graduate of the national FBI Academy. He's been the president of the Sheriffs Association of Texas, and he's a quick-witted humorist in constant demand as a speaker. He's also a licensed auctioneer and a connoisseur of Texas chili.

J.B. is also the co-author of The Christmas Day Murders.

Photo and Cover Photo by Randy Phillips Photography

Acknowledgements:

I've often said I couldn't track a bleeding elephant through the snow. But I don't have to; I have some of the best investigators in the state of Texas working for me. This is the story of two of them in particular, Joe Rasco and Pam Dunklin. They worked hard to bring the killer of this young woman to justice. This is their story, I'm just the storyteller.

I'd like to thank Roy Maynard for helping me to tell the story. I've enjoyed working with Roy, an experienced journalist and author, because he has helped me handle many difficult details with tact and dignity for all concerned.

I'd also like to thank our editor, Laura Krantz. She didn't pull any punches, and our work was all the better for that.

And finally, I'd like to thank the T.B. Butler Publishing Company for helping to make this book a reality.

INTRODUCTION

For there is not a just man upon earth, that
doeth good, and sinneth not.
Ecclesiastes 7:20

May 13, 2003

It's supposed to end now. The clunky ticking of the plain round clock can be heard over the hushed talk in the pew-like seats of the 241st District Court. The courtroom in the Smith County Courthouse is filled with staff from the district attorney's office, law enforcement officers, reporters, and most of all, family members of a young mother who was killed in her home almost a year before.

The defendant's chair sits empty.

Detective Joe Rasco can feel Judge Diane DeVasto's eyes on him. The clock ticks past 9 a.m., the time when this hearing was supposed to begin. It was to be just a procedural hearing; the defendant's lawyer – Buck Files, one of the best in the state – had negotiated a plea agreement and a 50-year sentence for his client. That client is now late for his hearing.

Judge DeVasto exhales loudly enough for everyone in the quiet courtroom to hear. She looks straight at Rasco.

"Find him."

Rasco nods, rises from his front-row seat, and strides to the door. He's out in the hallway when his cell phone rings. It's his partner, Detective Pam Dunklin. She doesn't know how timely her news about the defendant is going to be.

Joe listens for a moment. He's almost – almost – at a loss for words.

"Shit."

CHAPTER I

To everything there is a season, and a time
to every purpose under the heaven...
Ecclesiastes 3:1

August 2012 / August 2002

For a homicide investigator, walking into a crime scene for the first time is like being handed a jigsaw puzzle.

Well, that's not exactly true. At least a jigsaw puzzle has a picture on the box, and all the pieces. Homicide investigators don't have it so easy. There is no picture. And there are always pieces missing.

I'm Smith County (Texas) Sheriff J.B. Smith. And I'll tell you right up front, this book isn't about me. You'll learn a little about me as we go along, but this isn't my story. It's the story of how some of my top investigators solved a brutal and disturbing crime. This is their story, and the story of how a Methodist pastor's troubled marriage ended in the bludgeoning death of his wife. It's the story of how a case was built so solidly that the perpetrator of that crime pleaded guilty and is now serving 55 years in prison.

You see, in Texas, sheriff is an elected and an administrative position. You think it's about riding the range, rounding up rustlers? Think paperwork. Think staff management, jail administration and election cycles.

Like you are about to do, I watched this case develop. But I watched it from the inside, knowing I've hired outstanding investigators, and I felt confident in their abilities.

This story begins and ends with those missing pieces I mentioned.

We've never found the murder weapon – though we have some idea of what it might have been.

I'll introduce two of my investigators now – Detectives Joe Rasco and Pam Dunklin. You'll learn much more about them later, but for now, here's what you need to know: they're two of the best.

Joe is retired military who began a second career in law enforcement. He came to work for me in 1997. His direct supervisor, Lt. Tony Dana, says "he gets on these cases with the tenacity of a bulldog and doesn't let go." His calm, unswerving demeanor in an interrogation room is one of his most valuable assets.

Pam has an air of confidence and intelligence. She walks into a room and immediately, tempers are calmed. She can be the tough law enforcement officer; she can be the sympathetic ear. But it's her eye for detail that helps set her apart.

They're even better as a team. They talk through a crime scene together, remarking on what they see, confirming – or sometimes, more invaluably, questioning – each other's observations.

Their differences enhance their abilities. Their common commitment to finding answers and their patient determination to fit those pieces together make them formidable.

This book relies on their personal observations as well as the official records and reports. For Joe and Pam, this is how the "Unholy Ghost Murder" case began.

It was the early evening of August 5, 2002.

It was Joe's night to cook. His wife, Susan, was at the gym that afternoon, and as he drove home from work he wasn't so much thinking about what to cook – chicken (I'm not saying anything about his culinary repertoire, but they eat a lot of chicken) – as how he was going to cook it. On his police-band radio, he heard something about a call and a possible dead body, but he didn't think much of it.

Then he got a call on his cell phone, at about 6:30 p.m.

Pam, too, was on her way home. She was also thinking about supper for her family – Scott, her husband, her 6-year-old son, and her college-age twin daughters. She didn't hear the radio traffic, but she got a call on her cell phone, too.

Let me apologize now for what we can only call cop-speak. We don't really talk this way, but when I quote from written reports, you'll notice a formal, dispassionate tone, and some funny words. For example, in a police officer's or a sheriff's deputy's report, no one ever "tells" you anything. They always "advise" you. I've read many reports that must sound funny to civilians – a big, burly, experienced investigator will be "advised" by a 4-year-old that his mommy is coming to the door. I've never actually taken advice from a 4-year-old. Maybe I should.

But there's a purpose in keeping things dispassionate in reports. It helps you sleep at night. When you write down what you've seen, in precise and formal language, you can put it aside when you go home, knowing you've done your job as a professional. It helps keep things at a little bit of a distance. In a case like this, you need that distance.

"1830 received call from SCSO dispatch, homicide in Troup at 200 S. Virginia, single female victim," Joe's August 8 report reads. "1905 arrived at scene which has been secured by responding deputies. Detective was briefed by Deputies Stinecipher and

Grier as to the following: victim was Marla McCown Tabb, w/f, 4-25-67. Spouse, Michael David Tabb, w/m, 7-7-61, had arrived home approximately 1730 and found victim dead in the master bedroom."

What that means is that Joe received the cell phone call from the Smith County Sheriff's Office dispatcher at about 6:30 p.m. He was told there was a homicide in the small town of Troup, and he was given the address. He was also told it was a lone, white, female victim. Joe got to the crime scene at about 7:05, and Deputies Mark Stinecipher and Jackie Grier spoke to him before he entered the house. The deputies told them what they knew so far; the victim was Marla Tabb, she was dead in the master bedroom, and she had been found by her husband, Michael Tabb.

There was more; the deputies explained that Michael Tabb had told them he had been running errands, and had returned home at about 5:30 p.m. to find the front door open. He said he left his older child, age 2, in the car seat as he went in to investigate. After dropping a few groceries on the kitchen counter, he went into his bedroom and found his wife. Michael said he reached down and touched her arm and realized she was dead. He gathered up the 5-month-old child, who was in the living room playpen, grabbed the 2-year-old from the vehicle, and ran to a neighbor's home to call 911.

So far, that's all the deputies knew.

Pam received the same briefing. Standing outside the home, her initial thoughts were about how nice the house and yard seemed. It was a modest brick home, with a driveway at the side and a yard kept trim and neat. The signs of squalor my detectives usually see weren't present – the neglected swing sets or toys out front, the weeds, the broken-down cars, the broken windows and peeling paint. This was the home of a family that cared. Above all, Pam thought to herself, it was a home much like hers.

"Honestly, most of the cases we see don't happen in these kinds of homes," she said.

That's because when there's a homicide, there are usually other things going on, too, such as drug use or other criminal activity – things we don't like to associate with homes that look like our own.

"For me, it was how empty the house seemed," Joe recalls. "It was like walking into a cave. It was obviously the home of a young family with small children, but it was so silent."

Joe and Pam thanked the deputies and entered the home, switching into their tag-team mode. They noted that the front door – a medium-weight wooden door with a peephole and a deadbolt – was open, with no sign of forced entry. Just on the right, as they entered, they saw the living area, with a playpen.

"Please don't let there be a child in there who hasn't been found yet," Joe thought as they quickly crossed to it. They both breathed more easily when they saw it was empty, but for a big stuffed cow, black-and-white, crumpled in a corner.

They looked around the room. The walls and ceiling were paneling painted white – almost too white, making the room bright but a little harsh in the evening sun. The beige carpet seemed a mis-match, at least to Pam's eye. The television in the tall, sturdy entertainment center was off; the remote was on the coffee table, along with some folded laundry, a child's picture book and an unlit decorative candle.

The room was cluttered – but not dirty. There's a difference that any mother can tell. The couch was covered with a green throw, and it was full of folded laundry and a few child-size coat hangers. Above the couch was a framed studio portrait of a very young boy – an infant, with a baseball cap and a miniature baseball bat across his lap. On a facing wall, there was an old-fashioned cuckoo clock. On the floor there were a few toys, and a child's foam seat, upended. On another table, they saw a blood-pressure cuff and a stethoscope.

The living area also had a piano. Pam mentioned the folded laundry to Joe.

"It struck me how normal everything seemed," she says now, looking back. "I'm a mom. Folding clothes – that's just what moms do. I knew she (the victim) had just been doing the same kinds of things I do."

This is where the professionalism counts. Pam forced herself to remain objective.

They called out observations as they continued through the house. Windows showed no obvious sign of forced entry, either, and through the small, cluttered kitchen, a glass-paneled back door (through the "mud room," where small children and husbands can leave their shoes) was open. They crossed under a strip of yellow crime-scene tape in the hallway, and moved toward the master bedroom. They asked each other questions: "Did you see that?" "Where are the children now?"

The hallway itself was noticeably uncluttered. There were no pictures or hangings on the walls. The light was off, and it seemed dark, compared to the too-bright living area. Nearly all the doors were closed, or pulled to.

The master bedroom itself was at the end of the hallway. The first thing Joe noticed was a dresser on the right. It was a low, dark-wood "rustic" piece, with white ceramic pulls and a "country" plaid cloth on top. Above it was a simple mirror, with a frame that didn't match anything else in the room. The dresser had a few framed photos on it. There was a Bible, black with a well-worn look to the leather cover, which was engraved, "Marla McCown."

The bedside table was a bamboo piece with wicker drawers;

there was a white telephone on it, with upended photos and a baby monitor. It was switched off. Other photos lay on the floor, with their frames and glass broken. A lamp had been knocked over, its shade near the door. The bed was unmade, its blue-patterned spread heaped atop the sheets haphazardly.

Facing the door from the hallway was a bookcase; like most of the furniture in this home, it wasn't a match for anything else. That's typical of young families; it's what you would expect to see. On the bookcase was a small television/VCR combo and a cable box. Those were high up; on middle shelves there were more photos and some decorative crockery. The young wife definitely had a thing for "country charm" décor.

As Joe and Pam moved into the room, toward the foot of the bed, Joe began to note the blood spatters. They were spread across the wall behind the bed, at the far side, where the wall gave way to a curtained alcove, then met the far wall lined by a low, white vanity.

Joe's something of an expert on blood spatters. Pam had just come to the homicide division the year before, so he wasn't just making mental notes to himself, he was teaching Pam. He pointed out the blood spatter on the bedding and the wall; he talked about where the victim might have been standing when the blows came. A quick glance – for now – told him there was no obvious blood in the master bathroom.

"That means nobody tried to clean up," he said. That was worth noting.

The greatest amount of blood was pooled on the far side of the bed, beneath the body of Marla Tabb, who the detectives knew was just 35.

But I'll let Joe tell it.

"At the other side of the bed, detective (that's him, in cop-speak) noted the body of a deceased white female on her back with her left arm under the side of the bed," his report reads. "The area between the bed and the outside wall was approximately 3-4 feet. A large pool of blood was noted under the head of the victim. The victim's face was unrecognizable, (as) there were numerous gaping lacerations to the victim's face and head; it appeared she had been hit with a semi-sharp instrument. Several teeth were dislodged and lying on the floor. A scrape wound was noted on victim's right shoulder. Due to the amount of blood, detective could not tell if there were any defensive wounds. It appeared the victim had been facing a baby crib, which was in an alcove area at the victim's feet. One foot of the victim was lodged in the lower part of the crib. The victim was wearing a pajama top and short pajama shorts; the top had not been pulled up nor had the pants been removed. No shoes were present. Detective noted a large amount of blood spatter on the side of the bed, the outside wall, on the crib, curtains, ceiling, wall at the foot of the bed, and on the baseboard behind the bed. Some of this blood was cast off from the weapon.

"Other than the photos and lamp, nothing else in the room was disturbed and it appeared the entire attack happened in the area where the victim was located. Nothing appeared to be missing from the room nor the home."

Pam pointed out some significant details to Joe; there was jewelry in plain sight. On the dresser, a pair of gold-and-pearl earrings could be seen, along with a simple gold wedding band, a diamond ring and a necklace of small but authentic pearls.

"This wasn't a burglary," she said.

And she added that to her, the things that were turned over – the lamp, the framed photographs – seemed "staged."

These are the initial pieces of that jigsaw puzzle. And just like with a puzzle, you start with the edges.

"We work from the general to the specific," Joe explains. "We verbalize what we see, just in case the other detective sees something you don't, or sees it another way. That's the main reason you have two detectives on a crime scene like this."

With the scene as a whole taken in, they began to look more closely at some of those specifics. First, they examined the doors and windows more closely, looking for any signs of forced entry. All the deadbolts were working. At the front door, the deadbolt didn't even have a key; it could only be opened from the inside. The detectives talked about this. Would a young mother, perhaps alone with her children, leave the doors unlocked? Who would she have opened them to?

Joe also looked for traces of blood outside the master bedroom – the exit pathway the murderer would have had to take, in order to leave from either the front or the back door. No traces of blood.

But there was something; a dark pool of "brown liquid substance" at the bedroom doorway. It was mostly soaked into the rougher berber carpet of the hallway. It was too dark to be blood. Michael Tabb would later acknowledge this was where he vomited.

And as the detectives worked, they continued to talk to each other. "What kind of weapon could it have been?" "Where are the children?"

One of their observations, before leaving the crime scene to go speak with Michael Tabb, was that one of the children had to have been in the home – in either the playpen in the living room or the crib next to Marla – when that child's mother was murdered.

CHAPTER II

There is an evil which I have seen under the sun,

and it is common among men...

Ecclesiastes 6:1

August 5, 2002

The call comes in during a quiet summer evening, just after 5:30 p.m.

"This is 911. What is your emergency – police, fire or EMS?" the dispatcher, Rob, asks.

He hears a female voice.

"This man just came into my house. Says his wife's dead and he brought his two babies over here. It's at 200 South Virginia, in Troup, Texas."

Rob is already entering data into his terminal. He confirms the address.

"Two-hundred South Virginia? Do you know this man?"

She responds, "Yes, sir. He's the preacher at the Methodist church."

"How far does he live from you?"

"I live catty-corner across the alley from him," she responds.

Something's off; the address doesn't match the location the computer is giving for the phone call.

"You don't know his address?" Rob asks.

The neighbor responds, "It's 200..."

Rob understands. "That's his?"

"Yes, that's his address."

Rob is entering information into his computer as fast as he can type.

Rob is well-trained; he knows his first job is to determine the nature of the emergency, the location, and to call on various support personnel. He notifies the police, the deputies, and the EMS or fire departments if needed. He knows from his year or so on the job that this is a "hot call," something that will require all available resources.

"Did he say what happened?" he asks.

"Do you want to talk to him?"

It's an unexpected question. Rob doesn't hesitate.

"Yes ma'am. Is he there?"

He can hear the phone being moved, not merely handed off. He soon hears a man's voice. It's high-pitched. The man sounds out of breath.

"Hello? Hello?" the man says.

"Yes sir, this is the sheriff's office," Rob says.

"Yes, sir."

Today, Rob (who is now a Texas Department of Public Safety trooper) says he remembers the call for the calm, taciturn voice on the other end.

"The first impression I got was he came home and found his wife murdered – how horrible!" Rob says now. "But he was calm. He wasn't distraught like, well, I guess a normal person would be."

But on that hot August evening, Rob's focus was on getting information.

"What's going on? I mean, what happened?" he asked.

The man responds slowly. "I walked..."

He pauses and breathes heavily into the phone. "The door, the front door was open. And I pulled up to see where she was. I didn't hear a response. I went in the bedroom, and there she is, lying dead."

"Okay," Rob says, and he checks his screen again, as he receives information on the locations of the Troup police, the Smith County sheriff's deputies on patrol at the time, and detectives. He enters more information, updates what he has, and retrieves more information on the location from the computers in front of him.

His supervisor, Jana Bradley, looks on. Rob continues entering information. Jana soon goes to another terminal and begins entering even more.

After a pause, the caller continues.

"Someone had beaten her up," he says.

Rob still types. "What's your name, sir?"

The caller is taken off-guard. "Pardon?"

"What is your name?

"My name is Mike Tabb," the caller says. "T-A-B-B."

"Okay," Rob says as he types. "Did you check her pulse?"

"Yes," Tabb responds. "Yes sir, I did."

Rob turns in his chair, while stepping on a floor pedal that cuts his microphone. He sees another dispatcher looking on.

"Paula, get somebody started to Troup," he says. "I've got a lady that's been killed by assault. Yeah, this guy's a preacher in Troup. And he walked in and found her."

He turns back, then steps on the switch again.

"After you checked her, sir, did you touch anything after you left?" Rob asks – now a little flustered himself. "I mean, after you checked her for a pulse, what did you do?"

Tabb's words seem to get jumbled up now.

"I ran to my... I have a 5-week-old baby," he says. "I just grabbed the baby and I had my 2-year-old. We got out of the truck, and I just came right to the neighbor's house."

Tabb is breathing heavily again.

"What's your phone number at your house, sir?" Rob asks.

"My phone number? It's 842... 3... 3..." He breathes more sharply. "Sorry, I can't think."

"Okay," Rob responds. "What's her name, sir?"

"Marla."

"Marla Tabb?" Rob asks.

"Yes, sir."

"How old is she?"

After a slight pause, Tabb corrects the dispatcher. "Was. Thirty-five."

"She's 35?" Rob asks.

"Yes, sir."

"And you're a preacher at..."

Now Tabb interrupts. "The Methodist church, the First Methodist Church in Troup. My house is right behind the church."

"Is that an apartment?" Rob asks. Of course, he realizes it probably isn't; his goal now is to keep Tabb on the phone until the police arrive. Tabb doesn't know this. Or at least he seems to disapprove of the question.

"No sir," he says, sounding exasperated. "That's a house."

"Where did you come home from," Rob asks. Even now, the information being gathered is important. It could later play a role in helping detectives determine the timeline, for example.

"Uh, I went to, uh, Tyler and visited with my mom and dad, and then I stopped by the Brookshire's on the way home and I picked up some milk and, uh, and bread," he says.

Rob wants to keep Tabb talking.

"Okay, when was the last time you spoke to her today?" he asks.

"Uh, I want to say about 2:45."

Rob, in a hurry, forgets to use the floor switch to cut his microphone as he asks another dispatcher to see if the EMS unit is en route.

"Pardon?" Tabb asks. "Pardon?"

Tabb sounds confused, and almost irritated. Rob forges on ahead.

"What are her... I mean, visibly, what are the injuries, that you can tell?"

Tabb sounds matter-of-fact about this. "Somebody beat her with, looked like, with a baseball bat. I mean, she's beat up bad."

Rob again turns to his fellow dispatcher. He tells her the victim is Tabb's wife and the event occurred in Tabb's home.

"Yes, sir," Tabb says, confirming the overheard words.

"Okay," Rob says. "We've got people on their way, sir, just stay on the line with me. Just take a deep breath if you can. Are your kids there with you?"

Now, Tabb's voice seems to shake.

"The neighbor's got them," he says.

Rob is trying to fit together the information. "Where are you now?"

"I'm at her house," Tabb says. "She lives down behind us."

There's a pause; Rob thinks he hears Tabb sobbing. Rob's task now is to keep Tabb on the line, and (if possible) alert and fo-cused.

"Sir? Sir? Hello! Sir?"

"Huh?" Tabb answers after a moment.

"What... what was the last time you talked to your wife today?"

"About 2:45, 3-ish?" Tabb says.

"You talked to her on a cell phone?" Rob asks.

"No, sir... I, uh, I went, I was, I saw her, I left.. I, uh..."

"You left Troup," Rob offers, to help keep him focused. But he notices the false starts.

"When I left Troup to go to Tyler I picked up my son," Tabb says. "He had missed his nap, and he was cranky, and she asked me to just, just drive him around – he might fall asleep – and to pick up some groceries. And then I went into town, went into Tyler, to visit my mom, my dad. My dad had been out of town and he was coming back and I just wanted to visit them."

There's a pause, and Tabb changes the subject. "Who's, who's coming?"

"They've got EMS coming, and also it's going to be our vehicles and also Troup P.D. is going to be en route there."

Tabb asks, "Who am I speaking with?"

"This is Smith County Sheriff's Office," Rob answers. "My name is Rob. Just stay on the line with me. We're going to get you help coming out there."

"Is this the number to 911?" Tabb asks.

It's an odd question, but Rob remembers that Tabb hadn't dialed the phone.

"Yes, sir. You're on 911." By now, Rob knows the conversation isn't a typical 911 call. He tries to redirect it. "The door was open, you said, when you came back in?"

Of course, Rob has details of the call on the screen in front of him. He waits for Tabb's response.

"Well, no, the back door was locked, but, uh, when I was driving by I noticed the front door was open," Tabb says. Then, probably to the neighbor, Tabb says, "Yeah, they've got someone coming from the sheriff's office."

Rob tries again to focus the man. "When you walked in, did it... did you see anything cluttered, or the home was... like it had been ransacked?"

Tabb doesn't pause here. "No, sir, but the bedroom was messed up. I wasn't in the house more than 30 seconds, so I don't really know."

"Okay," Rob says. "And you're certain she wasn't breathing?"

Tabb exhales impatiently. "Yes, sir."

"She doesn't have any kind of medical problem or anything?"

"No, sir," Tabb says.

Sirens are becoming audible in the background.

"Have ya'll had any problems out of anybody lately, or..." Rob begins to ask.

Tabb cuts him off. "No, no. My phone number is 3531. I just remembered it."

Rob types, but continues with his questions. "Okay. The kids didn't go in?"

"One of them was already in," Tabb says. "He, he was in the... the pen, the playpen. I hear somebody now."

"Is that a portable phone?" Rob asks, not wanting Tabb to hang up until police are there.

"No, it's not."

"Okay. Can you... can you just stay on the line until you see them? When you see them, you can just go ahead and go."

"I hear a siren," Tabb says.

"Sirens like an ambulance?"

"There's... there's an officer right now," Tabb says.

"Okay, sir."

Rob takes a deep breath as Tabb thanks him. Tabb asks for his name, then says again, "thank you, thank you."

With a 911 emergency call, a series of events begins that could ultimately lead to the capture, prosecution and conviction of a criminal. That person could end up in prison, or even on death row. Dispatchers are far more than just glorified switchboard operators. They are often the first link in a chain of action, evidence and procedure. They must be alert and attentive to a caller's every word, every pause and every nuance. They must listen to and register the background sounds. Like all of my employees, Rob was one of the best, in my opinion. It's true, I may be a little biased. I'm proud of those who work in my department, and I stand by them for all the times they've stood by me.

But rarely does law enforcement encounter a scene like this. The violence, the anger, even the hatred betrayed by the evidence at Michael and Marla Tabb's home could shock even the most experienced officers. And amid all of that, the responders and investigators would be asked to put aside their feelings and perform at their best.

My team was about to be tested.

CHAPTER III

I applied mine heart to know, and to search, and to seek out wisdom,

and the reason of things, and to know the wickedness of folly,

even of foolishness and madness...

Ecclesiastes 7:25

August 5, 2002

I say "rarely does law enforcement encounter a scene like this," and if we're lucky, that's true. Don't pay attention to television; it's not one terrible crime spree per week (easily resolved within an hour). Small towns such as Troup can go years, even decades

41

without a murder.

In fact, in the whole of Smith County (which includes the not-inconsiderable city of Tyler, with a population near 100,000) has recorded less than 150 murders since we began counting more than 50 years ago.

My people have cleared about 80 percent of those, which is 20 percent above the national average.

We're often called in by smaller towns, such as Troup, even though they have an active and competent police force themselves. They simply don't always have the resources and the expertise we have.

Of course, my job is a bit more complex than the local chief of police's. My agency is not only accountable for the enforcement of all local, state and federal laws and for the protection of citizens and their property, but also for the delivery of criminal and civil documents, courtroom security, jail and lockup operations, and prisoner transports. My agency has to cover a lot more ground than just that within the city limits. And that stretches my deputies and my investigators from time to time.

As I've mentioned before, I think my investigators are special. I've told you a little about two of them, Joe Rasco and Pam Dunklin, but let me bring in another, now. His name is Pat Hendrix. At the time of the Unholy Ghost Murder, Pat was one of my top guys. Years later, he would retire from the Smith County Sheriff's Office, and take the even more thankless job as chief of police in Troup, which was experiencing internal troubles. It was even shut down for about two months due to a corruption probe surrounding a former chief of police. That was in 2006, four years after the events we're discussing here.

On that hot night in 2002, Pat arrived shortly after Joe Rasco and Pam Dunklin had walked through the house; it was about 7:30 p.m. The crime scene tape was already up. He noticed the church, just to the east of the residence. He also noted, with a sense of irony, that the home was also just a block from the Troup Police Department.

Outside the home, Pat speaks to Lt. Craig Shelton, who gives him the rundown. Shelton also tells him an interesting fact; that according to those he spoke to, the Tabbs have only been in town for about two months. Shelton also gives Hendrix the name of a church board member.

Another person arrives; it's Assistant District Attorney Jim Huggler. He's there to arrange for proper search warrants. He's in contact with Judge Randall Rogers.

Now, this is a small town. Word spreads fast. Already, bystanders are gathering. Hendrix sees all this and gets to work. His first order of business is to assign a deputy to start and keep a logbook that records the names, ranks, signatures, and times of those people entering and leaving the sealed area.

He's very clear in his instructions. No unauthorized people are to be allowed in (and as few of the authorized kind as possible). Family members, for example, often feel they need to be in the home where a violent crime has taken place. They sometimes even feel they have a right to be. But that's not the case. It's up to the deputy to explain to family members and others that by entering the crime scene, they could actually hurt the cause of bringing to justice whoever committed the terrible act.

Hendrix has switched fully into his take-command mode. He

44

talks to deputies and to the investigators. As he does so, he's amazed to see someone leaning against his car.

"Who the hell is that person, there, leaning against my car, in the baseball cap and the Texaco mechanic's shirt?" Hendrix asks.

"That guy? He's a member of the Troup Police Department," a deputy responds.

Hendrix doesn't like it. "I guess that's why he's wearing a gun. Get him out of here. Now. And I don't want any other detectives, any DA's investigators, or any alpha male supervisors here, either."

That's just how crime scenes work. Now, I don't know if too many cooks spoil the broth; I can't say I've missed too many meals because I counted people in the kitchen. But I do know too many feet, even if they're attached to law enforcement professionals, can spoil a case. The more tightly controlled a crime scene is, the more carefully the evidence is handled, the more solidly the case against the perpetrator is built.

Cops are curious; it's in our nature. New cops, especially, like to be where the action is. Even if they're not specifically called out to a crime scene, many will show up just to see what's going on. They'll call a friend, he'll show up, too. Luckily, that wears off.

"When you're new, you want to get involved in everything," Joe Rasco says. "But you learn very quickly that if your name appears in somebody's report you're going to end up getting subpoenaed in court, and after you do that a couple of times that puts a damper on the whole business, real quick."

He's right. As my detectives know, you won't see J.B. Smith at a crime scene until they tell me I can come to the crime scene. When they've got it wrapped up, I'll go out. I'll be notified, of course (and I received a call about the time Joe and Pam did). But I'm not going to interfere in my detectives' duties, if I can help it.

The crime scene at the Tabb home is still full of interested but in-the-way observers.

Huggler emerges from the house. He's ready to submit a warrant to Judge Rogers for a thorough search of the home. He's seen Marla's body, and the attack was so brutal that he can tell little. He wonders if a shotgun was involved; her face and neck could easily have taken a shotgun blast.

So when he prepares the warrant, he lists a search for "ballistic evidence including firearms, spent and unspent ammunition, spent casings and spent projectiles, holsters, silencers, and reloading equipment."

That's just in case a firearm was used. In the more likely event that Marla was killed by blunt force, he also lists "instrument or instruments capable of causing blunt traumatic injuries."

But to cover anything else that might come up, he adds, "any other evidence that tends to link any suspect to this crime scene."

He types these out on his laptop computer and portable printer. We're high-tech, even out here.

Meanwhile, more people are arriving. Neighbors wander over to see what the fuss is all about.

One of the best uses of all the extra cop bodies is to question these people. So deputies begin speaking to the neighbors.

One young woman volunteers some information; she'd been driving along Virginia Street and remembered seeing a fairly new model Ford Ranger pickup, green in color. She remembered that it was parked, with a window down, and the driver looked as if he was an older white male in his sixties. He was smoking a cigarette.

Where was he parked?

"In the parking lot of the Methodist church," she answered. "Facing the police station."

No, she added when asked, she couldn't recall ever seeing him before.

Another neighbor told a deputy about seeing a younger black male, probably in his thirties, walking from the area of a Laundromat to a nearby feed store. The neighbor who volunteered this information said the man seemed either distracted or drunk, because he almost struck him with his car when the man walked out into the street.

Asked for a description, the neighbor said he was wearing a white shirt, probably a T-shirt, and blue jeans.

The deputy rushes over to Joe to report these accounts; they could be significant. Heck, anything could be significant at this point in an investigation.

Joe, now standing outside, listens closely. He asks the deputy a few questions.

"Did he look remarkable in any way?" Joe asks. "If he had a white shirt on, there would have been lots of blood."

"No," the deputy says. "I asked him that, and he said he saw no blood."

The two are approached by Hendrix. As they start to compare notes, yet another deputy comes up to them.

"Sgt. Hendrix, we've conducted an outside perimeter search of the residence and surrounding area," the deputy reports.

That would have included bushes, plants, culverts – anything and everything, especially places where evidence might have been tossed or concealed. The search includes the area around the Tabb's home, of course, the alley behind it, and even a small wooded area nearby.

"We haven't found anything noteworthy," the deputy says.

By now, three more women have reported seeing a running man – this time, however, it's a white male they've described. But he's also wearing a white T-shirt and jeans. They say he doesn't look like a jogger; "it's like he was running from someone or something." About six feet tall, they said, with a ponytail.

"Lots of activity on this street today," Hendrix says.

Pam Dunklin joins the growing crowd of investigators. She mentions a couple of other homicides – the last one in Troup, five years before, but also a more recent one in nearby Overton.

"But those were two white females stabbed to death," she says.

It turned out that the Troup police had found another body today, she adds.

"But it looked like a suicide," she says. "The Troup police chief, Chester Kennedy, said he thinks the other victim has been depressed."

Hendrix frowns. "Talk to Kennedy," he tells Pam. "He may have some input. Or may not, according to what's been going on around here. I hear they're not keeping very good records."

He's more right than he realizes; and a few years from this awful day, he'd be brought in to clean up the mess left by Chester Kennedy. Pam leaves the group to find the chief.

Now it's Stinecipher's turn to approach the group. Hendrix turns to him and asks about Tabb.

"I found him in his Tahoe, outside the residence," Stinecipher reports. "I watched him for a few minutes before I went up and talked to him. To me, he appeared to be disturbed – but not really upset. Know what I mean?"

The detectives nod.

"I got his personal information from him," Stinecipher says. "His hands were shaking. I asked what happened, and here's his story. He says that about 3 o'clock, he and his 2-year-old had gone to Brookshire's and bought milk and bread, and then to the movie store, but they didn't rent a movie. He says then he went to his parents' house. Then he returned home about 6 o'clock. When he got out of his truck, he left his 2-year-old but he took the milk and the bread; he unlocked the door to the mud room, which leads into the residence from the garage."

The detectives listen closely; there are new details here, details that could confirm or confound an alibi.

"He said he also noticed the front door was open – even though that door always stays closed, he said," Stinecipher continues. "I asked how far it was open. He said wide enough to walk through. He says next, he put the milk in the refrigerator. He walked into

51

the family room, where he saw his other child, in the playpen, in a child seat."

The detectives frown, but continue listening.

"Then he said he yelled, 'Marla,' and got no answer," Stinecipher says. "So he walked into the master bedroom, where he found his wife. He said he touched her wrist. She wasn't cold but she wasn't warm. He says he grabbed his baby, then got his 2-year-old from the truck and ran to the neighbor's house, where he began beating on the door for help. He said he might have even kicked the door in. When he saw the neighbor, he told her his wife was dead. The neighbor then called 911."

August 5, 2002

I'm not going to preach. I can tell a joke, I can give a speech, I can auctioneer, I can even have a pleasant conversation with my wife.

But I'm no preacher. And I'm no theologian.

Still, there's one passage from the Bible I think applies here; it's from the book of Ecclesiastes (in the good old King James Version):

The thing that hath been, it is that which shall be; and that which is done is that which shall be done: and there is no new thing under the sun.

Why does this apply? As I look back over this case, the words, "there is no new thing under the sun" come back to me again and again.

Why was Marla Tabb killed? Was it a robbery gone wrong? Was it a random act of violence? Did she let a stranger into her home?

And what could explain the rage – the very obvious rage – expressed in the brutal nature of her death?

I was first elected sheriff of Smith County in 1976, and over the years I've become passionate about both my job and the people of my county. I've also learned a thing or two, as have my detectives. And the sad fact is that when a woman is murdered, the first people you look to are the men in her life. The murderer is far more likely to be one of those men, than a person she doesn't know. There is nothing new under the sun; you're pretty nearly always right.

That's why Detective Jackie Grier asks Michael Tabb for his clothing – his shirt, his pants, his socks and his shoes. A neighbor, who was also a member of Tabb's church, provides him with a change of clothes. Tabb goes into another room to change.

So far, Tabb is being cooperative.

When he brings out what he had been wearing, he hands the arm-full to Grier. Grier then takes the bundle to Stinecipher. They take it outside, into the fading twilight.

Deputy Mark Stinecipher is one of the best. I know I keep saying that, but it's true. When he reaches the driveway, he looks closely at the bundle he's been handed. At his side is Detective Tony Dana; they both notice what appeared to be blood on the shoes. It is between the laces, it is in the stitching. There's something else, too.

"Tony, that's a hair," Stinecipher says.

Tony Dana nods. There's a human hair on one of the shoe laces.

Another deputy, with a field test kit, confirms that the substance on the shoes is, indeed, blood.

It's time to talk to Michael Tabb.

Just across the street from the scene of the murder, the Troup

Police Department had a small interview room (it's now an office). It was a cold, stark room, with cinder-block walls covered with a heavy gray paint. A simple table stood in the room, and a tape recorder would have been placed on it.

In the hours since the 911 call, plenty of people had been plenty busy. Michael Tabb had been allowed to go to the nearby home of one of his parishioners, Gene Cottle. It was Gene who gave Tabb a change of clothes.

Detectives Joe Rasco and Pam Dunklin drive to Gene's house, just a couple of blocks away. Gene and his wife own the local funeral home.

That's why the detectives find it remarkable that even before they enter the brick home, Phyllis Cottle comes out to have a word with them.

"Michael Tabb is inside," she says. "He's not acting right."

"Not acting right?" Pam asks.

"I don't know, it's just..." Phyllis says. "I'd be in shock. Or something. He seems very cool."

"Nonchalant?" Pam asks.

"That's it."

The detectives glance at each other. Phyllis helps her husband run the funeral home. She's used to dealing with people in the midst of a crisis.

Soon, Gene Cottle walks Michael Tabb outside, to the detectives waiting on the driveway. Pam and Joe begin by expressing their sympathy. Pam calls it "doing their 'nice' thing" so that a suspect doesn't shut down.

"Would you mind coming with us to answer a few questions?" Joe asks.

"I have no problem with that," he answers.

And so the three of them drive the short distance to the police station, and walk into that office at about 8:30 p.m. And I truly believe that even as they entered, Michael Tabb was thinking through his story, perhaps even thinking about how he could outsmart these "local yokels."

What Tabb didn't know – but should have, if he'd ever watched any cop show or crime movie made in the last 50 years – is that this was just the first part of the interview. There would be a second. That thing about good cop/bad cop – it's true. And it works, just about every time.

Joe Rasco and Pam Dunklin are my good cops. Their job that night was to ask the simple questions. To get the story. And then to get it again. And again.

When Joe punches the button on the tape recorder, he re-introduces himself and Pam, and does the usual "It's August 5, 2002" routine, having Tabb himself confirm the facts, so that the tape would be usable evidence later.

"Can you give me some background on your marriage?" Joe asks.

"We've been married about five years," Tabb answers. "We have two children – one is 2 years old, the other is six weeks."

Pam's face betrays no emotion, but she feels her heart ache in her chest. Two babies, now with no mother. She thinks about her own children.

Joe knows his question hasn't been answered – not really answered. He asked for "background," not "basics." "Background" implies a lot more; was it a happy marriage? Was it a long engagement? Was there any trouble?

But he merely makes notes for now and goes on.

"Tell me about your day," he says.

Tabb pauses. "Well, I went to work," he says. "I was there by the time the church secretary came in, at 9 o'clock. She usually works from 9 to 11, Mondays through Thursdays. I just did my normal duties until lunch time."

"What did you have for lunch?" Joe asks.

"Well, I left about 11:15 or 11:30 to drive to Tyler, to the Olive Garden, for our monthly meeting of Methodist ministers. I got there about 11:45, I guess, and I waited for the others to arrive. But no one showed up. So I left. I went to the mall, because I haven't seen it since I left the service, and it was right there near the Olive Garden. I walked around the mall some."

"Where did you stop?" Joe asks.

"Nowhere in particular," Tabb responds. "Then I left. I went back to the church. It was about 1:30 I guess. The secretary had already left. So I checked the answering machine, the usual stuff. Then at about 2:30 I went home."

Joe makes a mental note of this. That would put Tabb at home at, say, 2:40 p.m.

"Go on," he says.

"Marla said she was tired and was going to take a nap," Tabb says. "I hadn't had anything to eat, so I was going to make myself a sandwich. But we were out of bread, so I was going to go to the store to get some. Marla told me to take our 2-year-old because he'd missed his nap and was cranky. Riding around always helps him sleep."

Joe nods; this doesn't show up on the tape recording, of course, but it builds empathy with the person being questioned. A suspect may even start to believe you're agreeing with their whole story, when you're merely nodding that yes, dogs can bark.

"Oh, I changed clothes," Tabb adds. "I put on, um, blue pants, and a blue Oxford shirt. And brown shoes."

"And did you leave the house then?" Joe asks.

"Yes. I took the 2-year-old in his car seat and we drove to the Brookshire's in Troup. But, um, we didn't go in there, because I remembered that Marla told me the Brookshire's in Whitehouse is cheaper."

Pam makes a mental note of her own; that's about 10 miles away; a good half-hour out of his way. Who would go so far to save a few pennies on a loaf of bread and a carton of milk?

"But then I decided to go to my parents' house in Tyler to visit; my Dad has been away and I wanted to see him," Tabb says. "I got there around 4 o'clock, and left about 5."

"And then where did you go?" Joe asks.

"To the Brookshire's in Whitehouse," Tabb says. "And there's a Blockbuster next to the grocery store, and we went in there, but I didn't rent a movie. Then we went into the Brookshire's and I got the bread and milk."

"And then you went home?"

"No; I stopped at the church. I wanted to call one of my church members and ask about her sick daughter."

"What time was this?" Joe asks.

"Oh, around 5:45," Tabb responds.

He takes a deep breath. "And then I went home. As I passed in front, I noticed the front door was open. Kind of. Partially, I mean."

Joe nods again. This part is coming out quickly. This is the part that Tabb had, perhaps, thought through.

"I drove into the carport, and I took the bread and milk, and I unlocked the back door," he said. "I went into the mud room. And I noticed the door from the mud room to the kitchen was open. I put the milk into the refrigerator – I can't remember what I did with the bread – and I called Marla's name several times. I went into the bedroom, and I found her laying on the floor next to the bed. I knelt down beside her to touch her arm, and…"

"Were you checking her pulse?" Joe asks.

"Um, no," Tabb says. "Not really. No, I could feel she was dead. So I got out of the bedroom, and I got the baby…"

"The 2-year-old in the truck?" Joe asks.

"No, the baby, the 6-week-old, um, was in the playpen in the family room," Tabb said. So I got the baby, and I got my son from the truck, and I ran to a neighbor's house to call 911."

Joe nods.

"And also," Tabb begins – but then hesitates. "Also, I guess at some point, I guess I came back to the house, and came back to the bedroom, and I threw up. I think it was in the doorway."

The mood in the room has changed perceptibly. But Joe and Pam know their roles. They don't press Tabb on the inconsistency. Not yet.

"Tell me about your time in the service," Joe says gently.

"Well, I was a Navy chaplain," Tabb says. "I was stationed in Japan and in North Carolina."

"Did you like it?" Joe asks.

"It was kind of hard on us," Tabb says. "I guess maybe it caused some marital issues."

"Was there any abuse?" Pam asks.

"No," Tabb says quickly. "Never. Never any physical abuse. Ever."

"Never?" she presses, but gently.

"No," Tabb responds. "I mean, I think one time I grabbed her wrists during an argument."

"What other kinds of problems were there?" Pam asks.

"I guess she didn't like my drinking," Tabb says. "In Japan, we'd have arguments. And I guess it was a problem. Sometimes we would have arguments, and then I'd leave home for a day or two and go to a motel so I could drink. So yeah, I guess that was a big problem for us. She complained a lot about that."

"You must have been under a lot of stress," Pam says, sympathetically.

"Yes," Tabb agrees. "You know, young children, financial issues. This career change."

"You mean leaving the military," Joe offers.

"Yes," Tabb says. "But, you know, it was a mutual decision. She didn't like me being away from the family on deployments."

"Were there other arguments?" Pam asks.

"Yes," Tabb admits. "Well, yeah, of course. Like in March. We were arguing, in the truck, and she claims I tried to run over her. She was just like that."

"She claimed you tried to run over her?" Pam asks.

"It wasn't like that," Tabb says. "We were arguing, and she got out of the truck. And when I let off the brake, I guess she was holding onto the truck, and she fell."

"In March, so she was pregnant at the time?" Pam asks.

"Six months," Tabb says. "So she calls her father and says she wants to leave me. She wanted him to come get her. And he started to; he got part of the way here. But then she called him and said it was okay, that we had worked things out. We always did."

Tabb pauses. "Can we have a break?"

"Of course," Joe says.

Tabb has clearly realized his story had gone in directions he hadn't wanted it to. He paces a little, has a drink from the water fountain in the cramped gray hallway of the Troup Police Department. He wanders into the hall, looks at a few of the posters and photographs on the walls. After a few moments, he returns.

As the tape recorder restarts, Detective Joe Rasco's voice has taken a new tone.

"Mr. Tabb, you have the right to remain silent," he says, slowly and deliberately. "Anything you say or do can and will be held against you in a court of law. You have the right to speak to an attorney. If you cannot afford an attorney, one will be appointed for you. Do you understand each of these rights I have explained to you?"

Tabb nods, then says, "yes."

"Having these rights in mind, do you wish to talk to us now?" Joe continues.

After a pause, Tabb says, "yes."

A person's Miranda rights are absolute, and come from a famous Supreme Court case, 1966's Miranda v. Arizona. Every jurisdiction can say it a little differently, but that's the version we use. We even add those two final questions, to ensure the person understands his or her rights.

I say they're absolute, but actually there's a public safety exception. If a statement is made (by a suspect) during a time when there's a danger to the public, it can still be admissible in court, even if the suspect hadn't been read his rights yet. That comes from a case in which a New York cop had apprehended a rape suspect; the suspect had an empty gun holster. The officer asked the suspect where the gun was, and the suspect nodded in its direction (this was in a crowded grocery store, by the way). The Supreme Court decided that because a loose gun was a threat to public safety, the suspect's statement (well, his nod) was admissible.

But that doesn't apply here. Everyone in that small interrogation room in Troup was calm, my detectives had things under control, and Michael Tabb was read his rights, true and proper.

I don't know why he agreed to continue the interview. Probably he thought if he didn't, it would make him look suspicious. That's just dumb, really. He already looked suspicious, or else why would he have been given the Miranda warning in the first place? And if he'd remained silent, maybe he wouldn't have just dug himself deeper in the hole.

Joe and Pam continue the interview for another half hour; that's the "again and again" thing I was talking about. You want to get a suspect's statement several times, so you can look for inconsistencies.

Pam begins to take charge of the interview. She notices Michael Tabb's body posture. He wraps his feet around the chair legs; he bends forward at the waist. He clasps his hands together.

"Can I have a drink of water?" he asks.

"Of course," Pam answers. She leaves, then returns with a glass of water.

"Thanks," he says.

Pam gives him a sympathetic, friendly look. As Joe leaves the room, she continues the conversation with Tabb – but not about the murder.

"Who is going to help you with the kids?"

"I..." Tabb doesn't seem to know what to say.

"I'm sorry," Pam says. "That was a premature question. You have a lot to handle right now."

Slowly, Tabb begins to look as if he's been offended.

"I don't have anything to 'handle,'" he says.

It's clear that this part of the interview is over.

Looking back, Pam says that interview was a pivotal point in her career.

"Because I was still so new in homicide, I was still in denial about people," she says. "I was still trying to wrap my head around it. Even while Joe and I were interviewing Michael Tabb, I had a gut feeling. I didn't want to listen to that gut feeling."

The problem was that the Tabb family wasn't that different from her own. It was a military, church-going family — and this terrible crime shouldn't have happened to nice people.

"I hadn't been in law enforcement long enough to know that I have to stop fighting my gut feeling," she says. "I didn't want to believe this man could do what he did to this woman -- what was left of this woman — what I saw. It was and is still the most horrible crime scene I've been in. The whole time we were talking to him, I admit I was looking for a reason to believe him; I was looking for signs that he was telling the truth, because I couldn't wrap my brain around the fact that a preacher could murder his wife, who'd just had a baby. How could that be?"

But it wasn't just a gut feeling, she says.

"He was textbook with all his body language," she says. "He wanted to talk about things unrelated to questions that Joe was asking him. He would lean forward and be 'open' when he was saying what he wanted to say, but when Joe or I would ask him questions that had to do with Marla's death, he would close up — for example, he would wrap his feet around the chair, he would turn away from us slightly."

Adds Joe, "He tried to control the conversation. Instead of fully responding to a question, he would only partially answer it, and then boom, he would be off."

These signs are very important. People, they can't hide "body English" and body language. Experienced detectives, after doing this for years and years, get those gut feelings. It's not something written in a textbook or something they've learned from the police academy. It only comes with experience. They just get that feeling that something ain't right. They know this son of a bitch is lying, so they'll go back through the same questions. Sometimes they build a rapport. And sometimes, like in this case, they rely on the good old "good cop, bad cop" routine. And it works.

There's another point I want to make here; Michael Tabb's verbal demeanor during the interview was damning. My detectives agree.

"Over the years, I've learned that people respond to tragedy in different ways," Joe says. "For example, people have a mindset of how a woman should act after she's been sexually assaulted.

Sometimes that's true, but sometimes they act differently. One woman might come in here and just have a regular conversation and show no emotion. Another one may cry through the whole interview. Another one may laugh. You learn that, sure, but still when your spouse has just been bludgeoned to death, you're going to feel something. And judging by Michael Tabb's reaction, he seemed almost relieved."

Pam was struck by his lack of curiosity, as well.

"He wasn't saying, 'oh my God, who could have done this?'" she notes. "He wasn't saying anything about what happened to her. It was just very odd. Even some of the scum-of-the-earth people that we deal with show some emotion when they've been involved in a homicide, or one of their loved ones has died. But he was just void of any emotion, any attachment to her."

During the interview, Detective Pat Hendrix had not been idle. He'd been listening in on much of the interview. He had also contacted the Federal Bureau of Investigation, because of the nature of this particular situation. The Tabb family had recently moved from another state; there could be inter-state issues to deal with. FBI Special Agent Jeff Block has helped us, and many other agencies in East Texas, for a lot of years.

He wasn't surprised to be called in on this one. And as an FBI agent, he would be a "heavy" in that interview room.

It was time for the switch. Pam, the ultimate "good cop," gracefully leaves the room, just after Joe does. She exchanges nods with Hendrix and Block as they enter the room.

Pam's night isn't over. She has one more task to perform. She isn't looking forward to it. But she is the right person for the job. She dials a number that Michael Tabb had given her.

"Hello?"

"Hello. May I speak with Sue McCown?"

"Speaking."

"I'm Detective Pam Dunklin. I'm in Smith County, Texas. In Troup. Do you have a daughter named Marla Tabb?"

"Is she dead?" The question is unexpected.

Pam pauses. "Yes."

"What happened?"

"At this time I just don't have enough information to give you,"

Pam says. "Her husband found her."

"Michael?"

"Yes," Pam replies. "Michael found her. The children are fine. They're with a neighbor."

"How did she die?"

"We're in the middle of investigating," Pam answers slowly. "We're in the process of finding out. That's all I can tell you right now."

They speak a very few minutes more; Pam doesn't press Mrs. McCown with any questions. That can wait.

"It was almost as if she was expecting it," Pam says now. "Of course, when the police call you, you're probably expecting the worst anyway. When you're doing this over the phone, it's incredibly hard – it's incredibly hard, any time you have to tell someone their loved one is dead. But this time, I was trying to find just the right words, trying to soften the blow, but before I could get there, she asked if her daughter was dead. I wasn't ready for that."

Pam hangs up the phone, leaving the murdered woman's mother to grieve.

The first order of business is for Pat Hendrix to read Michael Tabb a "consent to search" form, which allows officers to search vehicles and all other property at the home. Hendrix even hands the form over for Tabb to read. Tabb says he understands the form and he understands the nature of the search. Then he signs it.

"Have you been given your Miranda warning?" Hendrix asks.

"Yes," Tabb replies.

"Do you understand your rights?"

"Yes, I do."

"And you are willing to talk to officers?" Hendrix asks.

"Yes."

"How long have you been married to the victim?" Hendrix asks.

Now, I want you to notice some subtle differences here. While Joe and Pam asked their questions gently and often sympathetically, Pat Hendrix is in full "law dog" mode. This was a crime, there was a victim. And there most definitely was a suspect.

"It's poker," Hendrix explains now. "It's playing cards. You don't know what I have in my hand of cards, but I'm darn sure going to find out what you've got. It's watching a person's eyes. It's watching their body language. Lots of times there's bluffing. But in the end, only one person is walking out of there with the pot. And it's going to be me."

Has anyone ever tried to out-bluff him, to beat him at this game?

Hendrix laughs. "Just about every single one. But they don't win."

The interview continues.

"What clothes were you wearing at the church?" Hendrix asks.

Tabb pauses, as if he remembers saying something about clothes before. "Blue pants. A blue shirt. Button shirt."

"What kind of shoes were you wearing?" Hendrix presses.

"The brown ones, the ones they took from me."

Hendrix doesn't like the way Tabb phrased that. "Didn't you voluntarily give your shoes to the officer?" he asks.

"Oh, absolutely," Tabb recovers.

"OK, I wanted to be sure we're on the same page," Hendrix

says. "Are these the same clothes you gave to the officers?"

Again a pause. "No sir, I changed my clothes when I came home, and hung them up in the closet."

"What time did you come home and change clothes?"

"Um, 2:15, 2:30-ish. Something like that. The clothes I changed into are the clothes I gave to the officers. The blue pants and the blue shirt I was wearing are hanging in the closet."

"I know," Hendrix says – in a classic "poker" move. "I already talked to the church secretary, and she confirmed those were the clothes you were wearing at the church."

It's just enough information to make Tabb sweat a little more; it was to let Tabb know he wasn't being asked questions for the sake of information; he was being asked questions the detectives already knew the answers to. That's enough to make anyone nervous.

"Tell me about the history of your marriage. Was it a positive or a negative marriage?"

"It's had its negative moments overall," Tabb admits. "But overall I think it was positive."

"You had some fights," Hendrix says.

"We had a few disturbances over my drinking, and no one else was ever involved."

"You had to leave the Navy."

"I wanted to get out of the Navy, and Marla wanted me to get out," Tabb says.

"Do you recall an incident while at Camp LeJeune? Marla called her father to come get her, because you tried to run her over with a truck and kill her?" Hendrix asks. His eyes and his voice are firm.

Tabb's response is exactly what Hendrix is looking for; Tabb gets defensive and starts speaking quickly.

"No, it wasn't like that," Tabb says. "I missed a turn and she got upset and was screaming at me. I finally turned into a parking lot and told Marla 'shut up!' And she unbuckled her seatbelt and so I stopped the truck and she opened the door and got out of the truck and I didn't mean to run her down. I let off the brake so she would miss the door handle of the truck so she wouldn't get my son and I thought she was further out from the truck than she was, but the truck hit her and threw her into the front door and she hit the front door and fell down."

Tabb laughs.

"You think that's funny?" an incredulous Hendrix asks.

"No, I stopped the truck and got out of it and Marla got up and she said I could walk home. I said we were a good 10 miles from the base and I was mad. I started walking home, but then I checked into a motel."

"Mr. Tabb, you were smiling the whole time you told us that story. Do you think that's funny?"

"No," Tabb says. "I guess it was just hearing that I tried to run over her in the truck. And I know it wasn't like that at all."

"You know she told her Dad that you tried to run her over?"

"Yeah," Tabb responds. "She told me she told everybody I tried to run her over."

"When was this?" Hendrix asks.

"Around March. And she did call her father to come get her. And he did come, he spent the night, we all talked. It was just an embarrassing incident."

Hendrix knows this doesn't match what he said earlier. He lets it go for now.

"Do you recall any other confrontations at motels or hotels?"

"There was one time where we got into a spat and I just checked into a motel at the base," Tabb says. "She was angry and came looking for me. And the motel front desk called the MPs, because they were concerned. I asked the MPs if I'd done something wrong, and they said no, because even though I had had a few drinks, I wasn't driving. I was just in my room. There's nothing wrong with that."

"Was this a physical confrontation?"

"No. I only opened the door when the MPs got there. Marla left, and then the MPs left, but later she came back and we went home together."

Hendrix leans forward. "Were there any other confrontations?"

"No!"

Hendrix sighs for effect. "I am asking again because I've had to ask you twice if you had any confrontations with Marla and somebody else had to get involved, like her father."

"I don't know what you mean by 'get involved.' The police have never had to come to our house and take a complaint," Tabb says.

"How. Many. Times. Have. You. Had. Confrontations?"

Tabb shrugs. "Other than that, three or four."

"But you've had to restrain your wife," Hendrix says (and by the way, he's bluffing – he doesn't know anything about this, yet).

"A few times," Tabb says. "I don't know how many."

"Tell me about that," Hendrix says. "Because I want to know why you would have to lay hands on your wife and restrain her."

"She'd be hitting me," Tabb says. "I'd turn away and sometimes she would stop, but sometimes she wouldn't, so I had to grab her wrists and stop her. There were a couple of times in the struggle when she'd fall down, but I wasn't yanking her or pushing her or anything like that. I never raised my hand and hit her."

"Who was the last person to see your wife alive?" Hendrix asks.

Tabb pauses. The audio tape shows that the pause lasts a full 15 seconds.

"The person who did this."

"And when was the last time you saw your wife?"

"About 3 o'clock," Tabb says.

FBI Special Agent Jeff Block speaks for the first time since the interview began. "Would you be willing to take a polygraph test?"

"Yes."

Block takes over the questioning for a few minutes; this gives Hendrix time to regroup, to think through his strategy, and gear up for the next phase. Soon, he's ready.

"Mr. Tabb, this crime happened one block from the police department," Hendrix says slowly. "It happened one block from the church. The killer appears to have been full of rage. You can tell because of how badly the victim was beaten. Nothing was taken from the house. And people we've talked to say Marla would never have unlocked that door to let a stranger into the house."

Tabb pauses, not sure how to respond. "No, nothing was taken. And I don't know anyone who was mad at Marla or have that kind of rage."

"Would she have unlocked that door?"

"No," Tabb acknowledges. "She wouldn't."

"Mr. Tabb, right now you are the only person who is known to have a motive for killing your wife. Your bad marriage. There was nothing taken. There was no forced entry. You fit everything. You're the one with the motive and the opportunity, and you yourself said no one else is mad at your wife and would want her dead. You are the one with all the rage."

There's another pause. Then Tabb speaks. "Since you said I'm the only suspect you're looking at right now, I think it would be in my best interest to stop talking with you people until I have an attorney."

"Oh, I didn't say you're the only suspect," Hendrix responds. "But that's fine."

"I thought that's what you said."

"Everybody is a suspect. But that's fine if you want an attorney."

"Well…"

"Marla's not from here," Hendrix says, as if imploring Tabb for help. "Do you know anyone with enough rage to kill her?"

"I can't imagine anybody," Tabb says.

"Mr. Tabb, if you don't want to talk to us and you want to have a lawyer, you have that right. You can stop this interview at any time. I'm just trying to tell you what I'm thinking. I'm thinking, 'who else?' One block from the police department. Who else would she open that door for? She didn't know anybody. But like I said, you can stop this interview at any time."

Hendrix glances at Block, who steps in. "Mr. Tabb, you say you are willing to take a polygraph test?"

"Yes. Now I think I want to stop this interview."

Hendrix nods. Block agrees to take Tabb back to his parents' house in Tyler. It's 12:05 a.m. on Tuesday, August 6, 2002.

CHAPTER V

And I turned myself to behold wisdom,
and madness, and folly…
Ecclesiastes 2:12

August 6, 2002

My investigators realized their first task was securing the crime scene and the evidence they knew they'd find. They combed the crime scene, just like you see on "CSI." It was late on the night of August 5.

The property/inventory sheets say that a number of things were taken as evidence.

From the bedroom floor, the inventory sheet lists "1 broken tooth from bedroom floor; 1 piece of bloody tissue from bedroom floor; 1 bone fragment from bedroom floor; 1 broken fingernail from bedroom floor, 1 tooth from bedroom floor."

A second sheet lists the clothes from the bedroom. "1 pair brown colored men's shoes; 1 pair of black ladies shoes; 1 yellow envelope, Credit Counseling, containing documents addressed from Michael Tabb; 1 multicolored gift box containing 2 small stuffed bears and last will and testament of Michael and Marla Tabb."

Another sheet lists the clothes voluntarily released by Michael Tabb (the ones he was wearing): "1 sack with 2 shoes; 1 sack with blue shirt; 1 sack with brown socks; 1 sack with pair blue jeans."

Other sheets mention a Hewlett-Packard computer and a blue-and-white baby blanket.

And there's the first mention of a strange wooden table in the Tabb's carport; it's missing a leg. Detectives take note of this fact.

The inventory sheet says investigators took one of the three remaining legs.

Their work continues long into the night. At about 4:30 a.m., my office calls out one more of my investigators, Rutilo Quezada. He is told to meet with the officers at the scene of the Tabb's home. He is brought in to help take over the duties of simply keeping people out. Quezada is posted at the corner of Virginia and Calvert streets, where the police blockade now is. He allows a tow truck in to take away the Tabb's vehicle.

"Throughout the day, media personnel were at the location but keeping outside the crime scene tape," Quezada reports at the end of his shift.

At 11:19 a.m., Detectives Tony Dana and Jerry Black arrive to look for more evidence. Of course, Quezada allowed them in.

But when Troup Police Chief Chester Kennedy arrives at about 11:35, Dana and Black deal with him quickly and send him on his way. His role in this case is going to be kept to a minimum.

Quezada works his shift, and signs out at 3:30 p.m., turning the crime scene over to another detective.

The day after Marla Tabb's murder is a busy one for my lead detectives.

That's how it is on a murder investigation. It's feast and famine – periods of mind-boggling activity and action, followed by long hours of waiting.

"There are a lot of peaks and valleys," Joe Rasco says. "A lot of people think because of what they see on television that it's just boom, boom, boom, boom, boom. It isn't like that. I mean you'll go boom, boom, boom, boom, boom for a couple of hours, and then all of a sudden it just grinds to a halt and then you're just kind of standing around waiting for something to happen."

Joe says he's been up for as long as 40 hours investigating a case.

"After the first 18 to 22 hours, you really start having to grind," Joe says. "The adrenaline is pretty much gone at that point."

Pam says she's not that tough (though I believe she is).

"Of course, the older I get the harder it gets, but what keeps me going through the investigation is when we learn something new. We get excited. Your adrenaline starts pushing you again," she says. "That's what drives you when you're that tired. Otherwise we would just crash and burn."

In my opinion, most cop shows are insulting to real law enforcement officers. They show detectives working on only one murder case at a time; my people are juggling two or three cases at a time, minimum. Now, within the first 48 hours, they might be concentrating solely on one particular case — most of the time they've got it wrapped up in a very short period of time. But it doesn't all wrap up within an hour (allowing time for Viagra commercials). And, I'm sorry to say, there's no tattooed hottie wearing a miniskirt and four-inch high heels walking around in a CSI lab. That's strictly for entertainment purposes, and has absolutely nothing to do with reality. I mean seriously… Joe never wears high heels.

"Is it critical you solve that case in 48 hours? Absolutely not," Joe says. "People don't understand that. Working cold cases, I have learned sometimes it takes a long time to solve a murder case."

Adds Pam, "Sometimes time is our friend. If a case goes on

a long time, the associations of people involved sometimes become dissolved, and they're more likely to talk."

Joe and Pam knew they needed to know much, much more about the Tabb family. At about 11:40 a.m., Joe puts in a call to Melanie Owen, who is Marla Tabb's sister. He tapes the interview. Melanie lived in The Woodlands, a – well, I can say this, because I have no pretensions myself – a pretentious suburb of Houston, with a cement pond it calls a "waterway" and the campuses of quite a few high-tech companies.

"How often did you speak to Marla?" Joe asks.

Melanie thinks about it. "About two times a week."

"Did you know of any problems they were having?" he asks.

"I know several times, Marla told me about times he'd just leave, and go to motels, and drink, and spend a lot of money," she says. "The first time it happened was when they were in Japan."

Joe makes a note of that. But there is more he needs to know about Marla.

"Is it unusual that she was wearing pajamas?"

It seems obvious to Melanie that's a man's question. "No, it wouldn't be unusual. She just had a baby."

But Melanie wants to talk more about Michael.

"There was one time he told me he hated Marla and hated life and he talked about suicide," she says.

Melanie then goes on to tell another side of the now-infamous "knocking Marla over with the truck" incident.

"Did Marla ever talk about leaving Michael?" Joe asks.

"Yes. She did. But she didn't want to, because of the children."

Melanie wants to talk about how bad the arguments between the couple were. But again, Joe tries to learn more about Marla. Melanie gives in.

"She was hot-headed," Melanie admits. "She could be opinionated. "

"So she had a temper?" Joe asks.

"Yes, she had a temper," Melanie says. "And I know there were some issues between her and the church, the directors, I guess, about the parsonage."

"The parsonage?" Joe presses.

"Well, she didn't like it," Melanie says. "And that was causing some stress between her and Michael."

"The kind of stress that led Michael to leave the service?" Joe asks.

"That was a mutual decision," Melanie responds. "That was due to his deployments. Those caused the stress. After the thing in North Carolina, when he hit her with the car, Marla told Mom she wanted to come home to Texas. And she told Mom how Michael was a good father and helpful, and he kept his emotions in check."

"What did she tell you?" Joe asks.

"Once she told me about finding a Yellow Page ad for a call girl service in Michael's pocket," Melanie says. "And she confronted him about it. He said it belonged to a soldier he was counseling. And she told me that she found out Michael had a post office box, which she didn't know about in North Carolina."

"What's your impression of all this?" Joe enquires.

"Strange," Melanie says, after a pause. "I mean, it seems like things were going okay for now. Just a few days ago, July 27, I guess, I talked to her and she seemed happy. They seemed happy. And there are other strange things."

"Like what?" Joe pursues.

"I think it's strange that Michael would have a complete stranger call Mom to tell her about the murder. He didn't do it himself, you know? And Mom was told the baby was in the crib in the bedroom, not in the playpen, which is what Michael is telling everyone else."

These kinds of interviews aren't easy. Much of the information gained is what we'd call "hearsay evidence." If you don't hear something directly, you can't present it as evidence. It can be a clue, of course, and it can help investigators track down leads and put together that puzzle. But it can't be presented in court. But it was an important fact, and Joe Rasco knows it, that the stories are showing more inconsistencies. But he knows he has to stay focused on what Melanie knows directly about Marla and Michael Tabb.

He presses on. "Tell me more about Marla and Michael."

"I know there are several times when Marla interfered with

his career," Melanie says. "He thought of his new assignment in Troup as kind of a 'make-or-break' thing for his career. Oh, and there was a time, earlier, when Marla actually called Michael's supervisor in the Navy and lectured him. They were only dating at the time, and Michael later said that his supervisor told him Marla would be bad for his career."

"Go on."

"I know there were times Marla wishes she had never married Michael, either," Melanie said. "When she found out about him locking himself away, like in his office, and drinking. And there was another thing."

Joe's senses perk up – kind of like a doctor, who is about to walk out of the examining room, having finished with the patient, who hears, "Oh, there's one more thing…"

"There was a time, a couple of weeks ago," Melanie began. "Well. Marla said she walked into the bathroom and Michael was in the bathtub with the oldest boy. Michael wasn't sitting. He was on his knees."

"Did she see anything?" Joe doesn't have to add more to the

question. Its implication is clear, and would be better coming without being led.

"No…" Melanie says. "But then a few days later she found Michael bathing his son, and the bathroom door was locked."

"What did she suspect?" Joe asks.

"Well, you know," Melanie replies. "I mean, she was concerned enough that she called me about it. That says something. When she confronted Michael about it, he said the idea of him abusing his son was insane."

"Was there anything more?" Joe, like all investigators, likes these open-ended questions.

"Mom and I were worried that Michael might be abusing Marla, because she had a black eye once. She said she got it from hitting herself with a car door."

The conversation reveals quite a few things about interviewing witnesses, friends, and family members in a case such as this — beyond just the danger of "hearsay" evidence (we all like to pass along rumors).

The first is that when people are upset, their thoughts are rarely very organized. I take that back; even when they're not upset, their thoughts are pretty jumbled. I know mine are.

This may sound like a wife-question (and I have a few ex-wives who have asked it of me), but have you ever listened to yourself?

Really listened?

Try it sometime. Listen and see how many times you change subjects in the middle of a thought, or even in the middle of a sentence. See how often you pause, say "um," fail to finish a sentence or use the wrong word.

The art of the interview is keeping your interviewee on track. You can't be Jack Webb about it (you know, "just the facts, ma'am," from TV's "Dragnet"). It must be done gently. Melanie Owen was in incredible pain, experiencing heart-wrenching grief. Her sister had just been brutally murdered. Her brother-in-law was the clear suspect. Her two tiny nephews were motherless. It was no time to press her hard about staying focused. Joe's interview style is about as good as it gets. You listen, you express sympathy, and you gently prod them back on track when you can.

But a clearer picture of both Marla and Michael Tabb was beginning to emerge.

CHAPTER VI

*This is an evil among all things that are done under the sun,
that there is one event unto all: yea, also the heart of the sons
of men is full of evil, and madness is in their heart while
they live, and after that they go to the dead.*

Ecclesiastes 9:3

August 2002

This could get graphic. But the cold, hard realities of a violent
crime usually are. I have probably failed to describe half of what

Pam Dunklin and Joe Rasco and other investigators did at the crime scene – checking for fibers, dusting for prints, Pam reaching down the garbage disposal looking for evidence – but I hope I've shown you how well they work.

I'm going to have to be more descriptive now. But first, once the crime scene investigators were finished with Marla Tabb's body, it still wasn't ready to be removed from the scene. In Texas, only a justice of the peace can release a body from a crime scene. And on the night of August 5, 2002, Justice of the Peace James Meredith officially pronounced Marla Tabb dead, at 11:30 p.m., and released her body to be transported to the Southwestern Institute of Forensic Sciences in Dallas. Workers arrived from a nearby funeral home (owned, coincidentally, by members of Michael Tabb's congregation, the Cottle family). They zipped Marla Tabb's remains into a bag, and attach a tamper-proof seal. They then drove the 90 miles to Dallas.

The autopsy was performed in two parts; the external examination the next morning, at 7:30 a.m. The internal examination was performed on August 7 at 7:50 a.m.

"The body is identified by tags," the official external autopsy report reads. "Photographs, fingerprints, palm prints, and x-rays are taken. The body is received with the hands bagged."

What the report is explaining is that Marla Tabb's remains have been photographed, fingerprinted, palm-printed, and x-rayed. The fact that Pam "bagged" Marla's hands (encased them in plastic covers) could help to preserve any forensic evidence she might have had under her fingernails, from trying to defend herself. Her killer's skin cells or blood could be on her hands.

"The decedent is wearing a two-piece white and blue nursing garment designed for breast feeding," the report continues. "The bottom of the nursing garment has patches of blood and the top of the nursing garment has bloody shoulder straps and a bloody back. The decedent is also wearing gray panties. There are no personal effects or jewelry received with the body."

Then begins the physical description of Marla Tabb's remains.

"The body is that of a well-developed, well-nourished white woman whose appearance is compatible with the stated age of 35 years. Her body, when nude, weighs 160 pounds (72.6 kg) and is 63 inches (160.0 cm) long. The body is cold, rigor is fully developed, and the posterior lividity is reduced in amount, red-purple, and blanching."

That's talking about what happens to a person when they die. One of the first things that happens to a corpse is called rigor mortis. A chemical change in the muscles occurs, and they become stiff. It begins within just a few hours, and within 12 hours, it reaches maximum stiffness ("rigor is fully developed"). Of course, the environment affects this; rigor mortis sets in more slowly in cold temperatures, more quickly in hotter temperatures. But it can be a good way to help determine the time of death, if these factors are taken into account.

As for "posterior lividity," that's talking about how gravity draws blood downwards after death. The blood collects and coagulates in certain areas. It appears "red-purple" (and can look like a bruise to an untrained eye).

The report goes on and describes her hair – its length and color – her eyes, her teeth, and even the piercings in her ears. Her genitals are examined for signs of violence, but the examination "reveals no contusions, abrasions or lacerations" there.

The report notes a couple of minor scars (one is from a Cesarean section incision).

But then it begins to describe the injuries.

"There are 11 chop wounds of the head which have been arbitrarily numbered from 1 through 11 with no regard to severity or chronological sequence," the report reads.

Chop Wound 1 is at the vertex (top) of her head. It split the skin but did not fracture the skull. The second wound is a "full thickness, linear chop wound of the right side of the head."

Chop Wound 3 is also on the right side, at temple-height. This did fracture the skull.

Three more on the right side, then a wound to her mouth; the blow fractured both her skull and her jaw (maxilla and mandible). Teeth are knocked away. One is found in her hair. One is found in her stomach.

Then the blows start on the left side of Marla Tabb's head. They continue with similar violent results, with a final listed chop wound to the left side of her nose.

But those are just the wounds to her head. There are even more blunt force injuries to her neck, her chest, her shoulder.

And x-rays show that her forearm, her shoulder, and her upper arm have been fractured.

A full 10 doctors – all pathologists and medical examiners – signed the conclusion.

"Based on the autopsy findings and history as available to us, it is our opinion that Marla Tabb, a 35-year-old white female, died as a result of homicidal violence."

CHAPTER VII

There is no remembrance of former things; neither shall
there be any remembrance of things that are to come
with those that shall come after.
Ecclesiastes 1:11

August 2002

There have been very few violent incidents in Troup in modern times.

The city of Troup, Texas is a small town in the far southeast corner of Smith County. It's an old railroad and cotton town. Its streets were laid out by the railroad company way back in 1872.

"The International Railroad Company opened the Palestine-Troupe Line on November 9, 1872 and the first settlers of Troupe, or Zavalla as it was first known, came from Old Knox-ville and Old Canton," the town's official history says. "The town of Troupe, named after a governor or possibly a county in Geor-gia, was surveyed and the streets laid out by the railroad in 1872. A map of the town site was filed for record February 27, 1873. The original town map made by the railroad shows a plat dedi-cated for a school at the location of the current elementary caf-eteria building. In addition, while platting the town, the railroad reserved a portion of land for the City Cemetery and it was dedi-cated in 1873."

By now you've noticed the spelling issue; it began its life as "Troupe," but is now called "Troup." In 1909, the railroad re-quested the town drop the "e." No record seems to remain of why the request was made; perhaps it was to avoid confusion with that county in Georgia.

The quiet little town wasn't always so peaceful. Oh, things began well enough.

"January 8, 1873, a post office called Zavala opened at the community, with John R. Thomas as postmaster," the Handbook of Texas (a project of the Texas State Historical Association) reads. "Within five days the first town lot was purchased. Also that year, Rev. W. W. Brimm came from Tyler to preach the first sermon, and in September a temporary structure was completed to house the eight-member Presbyterian congregation."

Soon, Troup was a bustling place.

"By 1892 the town had 600 residents, eight general stores, four churches, and various millinery shops, saloons, physicians' offices, and drugstores; at that time it also had the hotel, a district school, a meat market, and a cotton gin and gristmill. The municipal government included a city commissioner, a justice of the peace, and a constable," the Handbook explains.

So far so good, but tucked away in that historical list is the word "saloons." According to Troup's own records, they actually outnumbered the business establishments at one point.

"At the turn of the century it is said that the business community was composed of eleven saloons and ten business houses," Troup's records say.

That means plenty of work for that constable, and probably for that justice of the peace. I know from experience; nearly everyone in my jail has some sort of substance abuse problem. I have nothing against a glass of wine or a beer now and then, but I've seen the damage that excess can bring.

When people think of Texas, they often think of the Wild West saloon towns; from the records, it seems the burgeoning Troup, Texas might have fit that image more closely than many of us could wish.

Still, it remained an agricultural community. Its main crop was cotton.

"At one time, Troup had five active cotton gins and the community marketed from 6,000 to 8,000 bales of cotton annually; some of which were shipped directly to Italian spinners in Genoa, Italy," the town's official history says. "Although cotton was king, other principle money crops were bell peppers and tomatoes."

But there was more in the earth than crops in Troup's future.

"During the 1930s, the local oil boom helped the community; the productivity of the East Texas oilfield made Troup an important rail town," the Handbook explains. "In 1936 the community had two schools, one with twenty-three teachers for 527 white students, and the other with four teachers for 262 black students. At that time the town had some seventy-five businesses."

It had its share of tragedies through the years; a fire in 1880 nearly destroyed the entire town (that's back when the businesses and saloons really were wood-faced). A second fire the next year nearly destroyed the business district.

But the townspeople rebuilt, and over the years Troup continued to prosper. It grew until it reached a peak population of 3,000 in 1939, but World War II took its share of Troup's brave young men, and the waning fortunes of the East Texas Oil Patch took even more, as discoveries were made elsewhere.

Now, there are around 2,000 residents. They're mostly peaceful, church-going folks. They have nearly a dozen churches, including the First United Methodist Church of Troup. The people of Troup are also hard-working; there are more than 100 businesses in the town.

Oh, there was a bizarre murder back in 1980, when a father, a son, and a family friend were charged with the murder of a Bible college worker. The victim, Keith Wills, was promotion director of Faith Temple Bible College. The college was raising funds with a fireworks booth near Troup. The men had come to burglarize the fireworks stand late at night; Wills was standing guard because the booth had been hit already a couple of times before.

The sad fact about that case is that less than $150 was in the booth. And everyone who worked in it had been told, "If anyone tries to take it, you just give it to them."

I like what the pastor of one little church (and president of that little Bible college) had to say later.

"We prayed for justice and then for mercy in the eyes of God for the guilty parties," Rev. C.B. Anderson said after learning about the arrests.

Even before the arrest, he said. "We prayed God to show them mercy; whoever they were, they will certainly need forgiveness."

Andrew Lee Mitchell was eventually sentenced to death for that crime. An appeals court ordered a new trial, so after 13 years on death row, he enjoyed a little freedom. He was out for about four years, awaiting a new trial. He even opened a lawnmower repair shop. But he couldn't keep clean. He failed drug tests and went back into lockup.

Yet another appeals court set him free again; this time he stayed out for only two weeks before failing yet another drug test. In 1999, about 20 years after the murder, Mitchell admitted he committed it, and went to prison. Because of time served, he was eventually released, having spent a total of 30 years or so in prison.

One point of telling this story is to explain a few little things. By cop-show standards, and heck, even by my own standards, my detectives had Michael Tabb dead-to-rights.

He had the means. He had the motive – the only motive. He was likely the only person who could have gained access to that home, without leaving any signs of forced entry.

His story stank. It was full of holes. It had inconsistencies.

So why, you're ready to ask me, did FBI Special Agent Block take Michael Tabb and drop him off at his parent's home – and not take him straight to my jail?

That's a good question.

It's all about our justice system. Michael Tabb looked like he did it. He sounded like he did it. He was just about the only person who could have done it, and absolutely the only person in Troup who would have done it, in a manner so violent.

But it takes more than that to build a case that will not only convince a grand jury (which hands down the indictments), but also a trial jury, and then inevitable appeals courts.

When any aspect of the case is flawed, a defense attorney can jump on that and try to create enough "reasonable doubt" to get a suspect acquitted. We've all seen it happen.

Remember the O.J. Simpson case?

But let me get back to Troup for a moment. I truly love that little town; I've talked with my wife about someday buying a home there. It's peaceful and it's friendly.

That's why Marla Tabb's murder came as such a shock.

CHAPTER VIII

I applied mine heart to know, and to search, and to seek out wisdom, and the reason of things, and to know the wickedness of folly, even of foolishness and madness...

Ecclesiastes 7:25

August 6-7, 2002

Joe isn't the only one working the phones the morning after the murder. Pam is back on the phone to Marla's mother, Sue McCown.

"Can you tell me anything about Marla and Michael's marriage?" Pam asks, after she again expresses her sympathy.

"They've been having problems for some time," Sue replies.

"What kind of problems?"

"Michael would disappear, sometimes, overnight," she says. "And Marla wouldn't know where he was."

"Yes?"

"And on the Fourth of July, I think, Marla found out about a post office box Michael had in North Carolina," Sue says. "This upset Marla because she didn't know about it, and he had mail going there when they lived in North Carolina."

"Do you know why he had it?" Pam asks.

"No... well, Marla said she confronted him about it. He told her he was going to take out a life insurance policy and he didn't want her to know about it. He said he was thinking about suicide, because he was depressed."

They speak for a while longer, and Pam is able to fill in a few more details about their life in North Carolina and elsewhere.

"Joe, we're going to have to go," she says, as she walks over

114

to his desk, which is far more clean and neat than mine has ever been.

Joe raises his eyebrows. He's not a talkative man; his facial expressions do a lot of his talking for him.

"To North Carolina. Sooner or later."

Joe nods. The keys to any problems between Michael and Marla Tabb would probably be found there.

"Well, I'm going over to the Olive Garden," Pam says. "I'll see if anyone remembers seeing him there. Yesterday."

"All right," Joe says. He's working on a timeline of Michael Tabb's day. He's also matching names to the phone numbers he got off the Tabb's Caller ID the night before. There are some local parishioners, as well as some of Marla's relatives.

Pam's trip to the Olive Garden is disappointing. When she arrives, mid-afternoon, she finds a manager, and asks who was working from 11 a.m. until 12:30 p.m. the previous day. The manager recites a few names.

"Are any of them here now?" Pam asks.

"Hmmm. No," the manager says. "I'm sorry. I have a different shift on now."

Pam pulls a card from her pocket. "When they come back in, could you have them give me a call? It's about an investigation into a death."

"Someone died?" There's some alarm in the manager's voice.

"We're just confirming people's accounts of where they had been," Pam responds.

Now, you might think Pam would be disappointed. But this is the routine, unglamorous part of police work. You interview dozens of people, even hundreds. You chase a thousand leads. You talk to many informants with no information. Out of 10 or 12 interviews, maybe one is helpful. The others aren't shown on television. The old detective stories would say "you gotta wear out a lot of shoe leather."

But heck, we're a modern sheriff's department. Pam wears rubber-soled shoes.

Pam arrives back at the sheriff's office (we call it the SO) by about 5 p.m. She goes by Joe Rasco's desk. She shakes her head at his questioning glance.

"No one was there who would have remembered him," she says. "They'll call. Or I'll have to go at lunch."

Joe isn't surprised. Lots of their leads are like this. But he has some news of his own.

"I got a search warrant," he says. "We should run it tomorrow. I've got Cecil Cox lined up. It's for the church."

Judge Diane DeVasto had signed the warrant; because of a discrepancy between what the church secretary said Michael Tabb had been wearing in the morning, and the clothing he'd been in when deputies found him at the neighbor's house, it seemed to be a good idea to check the church. The church secretary was one of the many people Joe had called that day. She hadn't been at the church long on the day of the murder, however. Perhaps Tabb had changed clothes, or at least cleaned up there.

Because the investigation is now shifting into a different gear, it's a good time to tell you more about Pam.

"Next to Joe Rasco, I'm pretty boring," she says. She's wrong, of course. But that modesty isn't false. It's the way she was raised.

Pam was born in 1962 in Fort Riley, Kansas, to an Army intelligence officer and a stay-at-home mother. She thinks of herself as a typical "Army brat," moving to bases throughout the world during her childhood. She's the third of four children. The family finally moved to Texas, her father's home state, after his retirement from the Army in 1973.

"I've been here ever since," she says.

In her view, she did "everything backwards." That's not how I see it. I see how her experiences and winding path in life have made her an exceptional detective. She can relate to any variety of people, from all walks of life, because she's walked at least part of the way with most of them.

She was married young and had children, and only then went to college, for example. She "practiced at marriage" (her words) a couple of times before finding her present husband, Scott, to whom she's been married for 16 years, as of this writing. She has twin daughters, who are college-age, and a younger son.

She had a few jobs, mostly in the medical field, before coming to the Smith County Sheriff's office.

One of those jobs is interesting, particularly in light of her present occupation.

"I was a surgical assistant for an oral surgeon for a couple of years," she explains. "I remember the first time I watched him perform surgery at the hospital. He was performing an odotectomy, which is the removal of all the teeth. It was simple enough, I thought. I watched through my surgical goggles as he plucked each tooth out. If you've never seen this procedure, the mouth bleeds a lot. All I remember is I kept saying, 'it sure is hot in here.' The next thing I remember is waking up on the floor, looking at my co-worker, in her surgical garb, asking me if I was okay."

This left Pam with a resolution to steel herself.

"I was determined to do a good job," she says. "I wanted to overcome the sight and smell of blood."

And she did. She assisted in many surgeries over the next couple of years. She helped with major facial traumas (such as those suffered by victims of car accidents) and even dentofacial osteotomy, which involves sawing the jaw in half and moving it forward or backward.

It made her tough.

"I really didn't know that in my future was a lot more blood and smells," she says now.

She also took a job once selling x-ray equipment. She was divorced at the time, so she was looking for something with good hours that would allow her to be home, as much as possible, with her then eighth-grade daughters.

"I'll tell you something," she says. "My daughters didn't really like the man I was dating at the time. So they kept coming home from school, telling me I need to meet their history teacher. I refused. But you know, I soon learned that children are pretty good judges of character. I gave in, and that's how I met my future husband, Scott."

The girls take full credit, of course.

"They were quite pleased with themselves," Pam says.

But you don't just marry a person – you marry a family. Scott's father was a retired Houston police officer.

"He began telling me his 'war stories,' and I was intrigued. His job sounded exciting, unlike my boring radiology sales job," Pam explains. "I liked the idea of putting together the pieces of a puzzle, of solving the mystery and taking the bad guy off the street.”

She put herself through the East Texas Police Academy –
working full time during the day, and taking classes at night, for
nine months.

“During that time, Scott took care of my twin girls, and our
eight-month-old son,” Pam notes. “He never complained once.
He truly is Superman.”

While attending the academy, and afterwards, Pam served as
one of my “reserve” peace officers. That’s an unpaid, volunteer
position that many newly graduated peace officers, and retired
veterans as well, take. For the younger ones, it’s a chance to get
some experience under their belt. For the older ones, it’s an opportunity to keep their hand in.

“I did it for a little excitement and to do something totally out
of my comfort zone,” Pam says. “I guess I had pretty much decided I didn’t want to become a full-time peace officer.”

Still, my people offered her a job as a dispatcher in 1998. Pam
turned it down.

“I knew it would require odd hours, and I might miss something the girls had going on at school," she says.

But when they graduated high school, Pam took a job with us, in dispatch, in 1999. I didn't keep her there, of course. In 2000, I moved her to the Criminal Investigation Division. She executed civil writs, seizing property, and sometimes children from abusive homes.

"The largest thing I ever seized was a jet," she says. "The smallest was a 16-month-old child."

In 2001, she began assisting with homicides. Captain Mike Lusk was commander of the Criminal Investigations Division at the time. He assigned Joe Rasco as Pam's mentor.

"That was the best thing that could ever happen to a rookie detective," she says. "I hung on his every word. And in fact, I still do."

She learned fast. She had to. In 2002, just two months before the Tabb homicide, she was called out to assist with a drug deal that had gone bad. A young man was killed. In her own words, she was just innocently following Joe Rasco around, looking for direction in how to conduct an investigation, when Lusk approached her.

"Welcome to Homicide," Lusk said. "This one's yours."

"I remember how my eyes got wide, and I looked to Joe, as if to say, 'dear God, don't leave me now,'" she says.

It wasn't an open-and-shut case. There were five suspects. She had to travel to Kentucky in pursuit of leads.

"I wanted Joe to go with me, and make sure I was doing everything I should be doing, working the case like it needed to be worked," Pam says. "He didn't. But, you know, that turned out to be a good thing. I was forced to rely on my training. I learned to feel confident in my own abilities, without Joe to lean on."

Thanks to her work, and the work of others in my department, all five suspects are now in prison.

"I have Joe to thank for that," she says. "He's the one who gave me the knowledge and confidence to be the lead investigator on that case."

She now says that maybe Capt. Mike Lusk wouldn't have given her the case, had he known how complex it was going to be.

I disagree. She was obviously the right person for the task, just as her contribution to the Marla Tabb murder was crucial.

A few years later, she left my department to "pursue options." I don't begrudge that of anyone, but I don't mind saying I missed her.

Within a few months, however, she called me. The conversation started with just a few pleasantries, but once those were out of the way, I got down to business.

"Would you be interested in returning to the Smith County homicide division?" I asked.

But I'd known Pam Dunklin too long to just make her a business proposition like that. I ended with, "It's time to come home. This is where you belong."

She accepted, and she's been back in homicide, partnered with her friend and mentor, Joe Rasco, ever since. She's now achieved the rank of sergeant.

Others were busy on August 6, as well. Lt. Tony Dana and Detective Jerry Black returned to the crime scene in the daylight, to better conduct a search of the outside. But look as hard as they could, they found no new evidence.

Dana found himself in Troup yet again on the morning of August 7. This time, he was there to get a description of the church itself. No, the church was not a suspect – Joe needed a description of the church grounds in order to obtain a search warrant. That's part of an investigator's duties; it's part of the Fourth Amendment.

The Fourth Amendment of the U.S. Constitution reads,

"The right of the people to be secure in their persons, houses, papers, and effects, against unreasonable searches and seizures, shall not be violated, and no Warrants shall issue, but upon probable cause, supported by Oath or affirmation, and particularly describing the place to be searched, and the persons or things to be seized."

Now, here in Texas we're pretty big on our Second Amendment rights. We love to keep and bear arms. But as a sheriff, I know the Fourth Amendment is pretty important, too. Those old cop shows and movies that have law enforcement officials grousing about search warrants and Miranda warnings and such just aren't very accurate. We like knowing the rules, and we follow them closely to ensure the bad guys don't walk free.

But while Lt. Dana was at the church, he was approached by Gene Cottle, the funeral home owner who was also a member of First Methodist. Cottle told him that Pam had asked him to provide his shoes (and his wife's shoes) because they had been at the crime scene on the night of the murder, when they collected Marla Tabb's body to take it to Dallas for the autopsy. He handed the shoes, in brown paper bags, to Dana.

Then Dana was approached by two more church members, who said they needed to get into the church to get supplies for a memorial service for Marla, to be held the following Sunday.

Dana called Joe. The church members needed their address list so they could send letters to the congregation, informing them of the service.

"No," Joe responded. "Don't let all of them in. You can let the church secretary in to the office, just for a few minutes."

As Dana watched, the church secretary started the computer, and printed out the members' addresses onto sheets of labels. She gathered blank newsletter paper, blank bulletin paper, and stamps. It took less than 15 minutes, and when they left, Dana secured the scene.

Pam Dunklin, Joe Rasco and, another investigator, Cecil Cox, didn't get out to the First United Methodist Church of Troup until about 6 p.m. on that day, August 7. The search was routine. The small church office was the focus; Joe collected some bank documents.

They searched the small church office; the carpet was darker than the carpet in the Tabb's home, but not so dark you'd miss blood stains, if they were there. They looked in closets, in drawers, under desks. They combed over the small restroom.

Cox did some of the most interesting work at the site. As Joe and Pam stood back, he employed a chemical called "luminol" to search for traces of blood.

Luminol is an amazing chemical. A lot of criminals, even (or especially) very careful criminals wish it didn't exist. It's a white or yellow chemical that exhibits "chemiluminescence" when it comes in contact with an oxidizing agent – namely, the iron in blood. It gives off a striking blue glow.

To use it, detectives and crime scene investigators spray it evenly over a surface. If there's blood there, it will glow briefly (for about 30 seconds). Investigators can document this with crime scene photographs.

But Cox found nothing on that hot summer evening. The church was clean. If Michael Tabb had stopped in, after his wife's murder, he hadn't cleaned up in the church's bathroom.

CHAPTER IX

For to him that is joined to all the living there is hope…
Ecclesiastes 9:4

August 2002

In this business, you find relationships are key. And as the investigation continued, Joe Rasco and Pam Dunklin knew that they would have to start focusing on the relationship between Michael and Marla Tabb.

The best source for this information, of course, would be

those close to the couple. Over the next few days and weeks, my detectives spoke with Marla's sister and brother-in-law extensively, at one point even traveling to Magnolia, Texas (where Marla's brother-in-law, Tim, worked, though they lived in The Woodlands), in order to speak with them. I want to tell you about those conversations now, although they're not in strict chronological order.

"Mike's mom called," Melanie reported in one of those. She was speaking of the night of the murder. "I asked her what happened, and she said she didn't know. She said Mike had come home and found Marla. I asked how Marla died, and she said she didn't know. I asked her where and how Mike had found Marla, and she just handed the phone to Mike. I asked Mike what had happened, and he said he didn't know."

The frustration in Melanie's voice became apparent.

"I asked how Marla had died, and he said she had been beaten to death," Melanie continued. "I asked if the house had been broken into, and he said the front door was unlocked. I asked where the older boy was, and he said he was with him. I asked where the younger was, and he said he was in the crib. Then he said the police would be at the house all night. I told him we were going to get Mom and come in the morning. He asked if I had his parents' phone number. I gave the phone to Tim while I checked to see if I had that number."

Tim reported that Mike told him essentially the same story, and said he didn't know anything else.

The next day, Melanie reported, "Tim called Mike after our interviews with detectives. He told Mike we needed to make some type of funeral arrangements. Mike said that we could do whatever we wanted to do. Tim told him that we wanted to have the funeral in Beaumont, at Woodland Pines Baptist Church, and bury her in the family cemetery, which is Wood Cemetery in Pineland."

Michael Tabb passively agreed, she said.

"The only thing he asked was if we could get the preacher that married them to do the service, alongside the current preacher at Woodland. Mike never asked how any of us were doing – Marla's sister, her mother, her father. He never asked anything. He never expressed any grief or emotion at all."

Tim and Melanie Owen prove to be a solid source of background information on Marla and Michael Tabb's relationship. Tim spoke about Easter weekend 2002, when the couple was still in North Carolina.

"Marla called Saturday morning," Tim said. "I think Mike had left Friday, if not before. They had had an argument on the way to Red Lobster. I think this is the time that Mike tried to leave Marla in the parking lot, but she was in the way of the truck and the door hit her. She was six months pregnant at the time. It was either this time or the Mother's Day incident. Mike did leave — Mom and I think it was in a cab. Mike stayed gone from Friday night through most, if not all, of Easter Day."

Mike was then working as a chaplain, not a pastor, so he had no Easter Day duties.

"We don't know if he came back that night or Monday," Tim went on. "Marla was upset because all of their son's Easter stuff was in Mike's office, so he didn't get to have Easter. Mike spent about $800 on a hotel and cabs and could not account for $400

132

he spent during his time away."

The incident was a revelation to the family, Tim said.

"I think this was the first time Melanie or Mom found out about the ongoing problems Marla and Mike were having," he said. "Marla told Melanie that this wasn't the first time it had happened. She said Mike had done this a lot throughout their marriage. She said he went off and drank. She said she had told his family he had a drinking problem. Melanie told Marla they should get counseling. Marla said they had tried, but Mike just sat there and wouldn't say anything during the session."

Tim repeated the story about the Yellow Pages listing for escorts that Marla had found in Michael's pocket.

"But Mike said he had taken it up from one of the guys that he counseled," Tim said.

Joe asked him about Mother's Day – had something happened then? Tim responded that yes, it was another time that Michael had left, with no warning and no explanation.

"We're not sure what day he left, but he left in the truck, with their son's car seat, and he took the keys to the car, so Marla was stranded," Tim explained. "She and the baby both had doctor's appointments that week. She was having problems with her pregnancy – she had some condition that made her pubic bones separate and caused a lot of pain, as well as low blood pressure.

That explained the blood pressure cuff and stethoscope my detectives found in the Tabb home.

"Her doctor was so concerned that she sent a nurse to pick up Marla," Tim continued. "Marla must have confided quite a bit to the doctor, because the doctor was so upset, she wanted to take Marla to the airport to fly home to Texas. I'm pretty sure Marla couldn't fly because her son had ear infections at this time."

Gene McCown, however, was determined to come get his daughter and bring her home.

"Dad drove to get Marla, but Mike came home before Dad got there," Tim said. "Dad said that he talked with Mike alone. He asked Mike if he knew he had a drinking problem. Mike admitted that he did. According to Dad, Mike said that he thought things would change after he got out of the military. Dad said that Mike told him that with the help of a good woman, getting out of the military, having the support of my family, and this new baby, he thought he would be okay."

"What else can you remember about that weekend?" Joe asked.

"Marla told Melanie she was tired of covering up for Mike," Tim responded. "I think this is the time that she called his work, and he hadn't gone to work. He had an unauthorized absence. It was either this time or the Easter time, but I'm pretty sure it was this time. I don't know what all she told his superiors."

Tim and Melanie, together, then talked about a visit Michael and Marla paid them in May 2002, at their home in The Woodlands.

"I noticed a difference in Mike's attitude toward Marla," Melanie said. "Of course, we hadn't seen them together much. We had seen them in February 2002, when they came to Texas for my grandmother's funeral. But before that, we hadn't seen them since May 2001. But Mike really seemed to dislike Marla. He talked to her with exaggerated patience. It was patronizing, or condescending. He seemed to roll his eyes at her a lot."

Tim offered his memory of that weekend.

"Mike and I went on the back porch and talked about Troup, and being out of the Navy," Tim said. "He said that this church would make or break his career. He said that Marla disliked the town and the people she had met. She was upset that they wouldn't let her paint the house. He said that he hoped she would not screw up this opportunity, or they would always be stuck in a small town. He seemed pretty disgusted and fed up with her. I said that it was like a stepping stone, and she needed to understand that it would not be forever."

It wasn't the first time Michael said Marla had caused friction, Tim said.

"Mike told her she had angered the people in their church in North Carolina and they didn't like her," Tim explained. "He also told me he could not go to the commissary with Marla because she embarrassed him every time they went by the way she talked to people. He also told me she was very negative about the move. He was not happy with her."

Tim then spoke of a visit he and Melanie had paid to the Tabbs in Troup, on June 29 (just after the birth of their second son).

136

This was in June 2002, after the Tabbs came to Texas permanently.

"We visited Mike and Marla in Troup," Tim said. "We brought a cake and balloon for Mike's birthday. That was Sue's — their Mom's — idea. The only time Mike and I talked alone was in the bedroom, when he told me, "You would not believe the shit she has already pulled.' He did not go into detail because we were called back into the other room. We never talked alone again. Mike was not very talkative for the rest of the day."

That Fourth of July incident came up, as Tim and Melanie talked about the Tabbs' relationship. That had been the previous year —remember, people tend to jump around when they speak.

"Marla was considering leaving Mike," Melanie said. "Some man from an investment place called and said some mail had come back to him. Marla asked what address he had sent it to. He gave her a P.O. box in North Carolina. When Marla confronted him about this, Mike claimed he got the P.O. box because he was going to get life insurance and then kill himself. She didn't want him to get the life insurance, he said, so he got the secret box so he could get it secretly. Marla wanted to know why I thought he might have gotten a box."

Marla was considering leaving Michael, she repeated.

"Marla was extremely upset and wanted to come home to Mom's," Melanie said. "Unfortunately, Mom and I discouraged her because the baby was only two weeks old. Marla told me she was miserable. She said she didn't even know who Mike was — he had so many secrets. When she confronted him about things, his excuses never made any sense. She said that he told her he hated her, he called her a bitch, he said he hated their life and he talked about killing himself often."

Joe asked about the July 2002 incident in the bathroom, when Michael was bathing the 2-year-old.

"Marla called me and was concerned about Mike bathing their son," Melanie said. "Mike always took a bath with him. She said that she had walked into the bathroom unexpectedly and Mike sat up quickly and looked and acted very weird. She said his butt was not on the tub floor. He said he was washing his private parts. She thought that was weird, so the next day when he was bathing him, she tried to walk in unexpectedly, but Mike had the bathroom door locked. When she asked him why it was locked, he said he didn't know that it was. Marla wanted to know if I thought Mike was molesting his son. She was very concerned about it. I told her I didn't have any experience with that and I didn't feel comfortable giving an opinion. I told her to start bathing their son herself."

Marla was worried that Michael spent so much time alone with the 2-year-old, Melanie said.

"She was really concerned because she felt like she just didn't know what kind of person Mike was at all," Melanie said. "He had so many secrets; she just didn't trust him at all."

The Owens, Tim and Melanie, scrounged their memories for other incidents; there was a time, when Michael was staying with them for a weekend conference in Houston, when Michael didn't come home for the night.

"He didn't call or anything," Tim said. "He said he stayed with a friend."

That was in May 2001, they recalled. In 2000, just after their first son's birth, the Tabbs stayed with Sue McCown, Marla's mother. One night, he didn't return from a conference in Galveston to Sue's Beaumont home. He later said a friend had a hotel room in Galveston, and didn't need it – so he used it.

A much earlier incident occurred in Rhode Island, before the Tabbs were even married (their wedding was in Beaumont, Texas, on May 8, 1998).

"Mike was training for the military," Melanie explained. "The entire group of chaplains were going to either Boston or Philadelphia during their down time. Mike told Marla he wanted to go too. He pretended like he went. Somehow, she found out he didn't. He admitted that he had just holed up and drank."

Neither knew much about Michael's life or his relationship with Marla before the marriage, other than the fact they'd met at church. Michael never talked much about himself – or at least, about his background.

Maybe you're thinking about what I said earlier – about hearsay. And you're right. Little of what Marla's sister and brother-in-law said could be entered as evidence. But it was valuable nonetheless, as it helped my detectives to understand Michael and Marla Tabb's marriage. It was clearly troubled. Now, we just had to find out if it was so troubled that Michael Tabb felt there was only one way out of it.

CHAPTER X

Wisdom is better than weapons of war:
but one sinner destroyeth much good.
Ecclesiastes 9:18

August 2002

Other important conversations were taking place. With the feds now involved, two were sent to interview Michael Tabb's parents in Tyler. FBI Special Agent Cliff Carruth and Deputy U.S. Marshal John M. Garrison arrived at the home of Lloyd and

June Tabb just after midnight on August 6. Their reports were sent over the following day.

Special Agent Carruth led the interview with June Tabb. He went through the preliminaries, stating his name and the reason for the interview. He introduced Deputy U.S. Marshal Garrison.

Mrs. Tabb told Carruth her son had been married to Marla for about four years. She said the relationship was "good."

"She has never known them to have any problems, and believes them to be very happy together," Carruth's report reads. "Michael met Marla in Beaumont, Texas, in 1994, when Michael was the pastor of a church there. Michael entered the Navy and worked as a Naval Chaplain for approximately four and a half years."

Mrs. Tabb explained that when Michael and Marla moved back to Texas, they lived with her for about two weeks, presumably as the parsonage was being readied. They moved into it in either May or June – she couldn't recall exactly.

Mrs. Tabb "said that she saw Michael earlier this day when he and her grandson came to her house at approximately 4 p.m.," the report continues. "Michael told her that he was driving her grandson around, trying to get him to sleep. She said the child, who is approximately 2 years of age, has difficulty sleeping. Michael will drive him around in an attempt to make him sleepy for a nap. The child had fallen asleep and Michael came to her house to visit. When Michael arrived, he brought the child, who slept while they visited. She described their conversation as being normal, talking about general life. Michael told her he was supposed to go to a Methodist pastors' meeting at the Olive Garden for a luncheon. He arrived at the Olive Garden and there was no one there. He told her he guessed that the meeting had been canceled and that he had not been notified. This would have been the first meeting that he would have attended due to the fact that their children were small and he was not able to attend the meetings."

Michael did not appear to be under any stress or duress, the agent noted.

"They discussed the fact that Marla was going to join the choir in the near future, due to the fact that the church was going to start a new choir," the report states. "She states that Michael stayed for about an hour and left at 5 p.m. She remembers this due to the fact that her husband woke up about 5:05 or 5:10 and Michael had just left. Michael had told her that he was going to Brookshire's grocery store to buy some bread and milk and then was planning to return home. Michael was driving his blue pickup truck."

Less than an hour later, June Tabb and her husband Harold learned of Marla's death.

"She stated that at about 6 p.m., one of the church members, by the name of Trey (last name unknown), called and told her that Marla had been killed and that she and her husband were requested to go to meet with Michael," Carruth's report reads.

He asked about the last time the couple had seen their daughter-in-law.

"She stated that on Friday, August 2, 2002, Michael, Marla and the children came to her house where they visited," the report says. "Everything seemed fine in their discussions, and there did not seem to be any problems between the two of them. On Saturday, August 3, 2002, she met with Michael, Marla and the children for lunch. She described their visit as being very pleasant and not stressful. On Sunday, August 4, 2002, she spoke with Marla on the telephone. Marla told her she was having a neck problem but it was getting better. She also spoke with Michael at the same time on the phone but he seemed to be very busy with the church."

Carruth got some contact information for Marla's relatives (something other officers had also done, from other sources, but it never hurts to be sure).

"Mrs. Tabb stated that neither Michael nor Marla had told her anything about any suspicious people or any problems with anyone in the neighborhood," Carruth's report concludes. "The murder of Marla is a complete surprise and she does not know who would have killed Marla, for any reason."

When it was time to interview Harold Lloyd Tabb, Garrison took the lead.

Mr. Tabb spoke of how Michael and Marla met.

"Mike and Marla met when they were both campaigning for U.S. Congressman Steve Stockman," Garrison's report explains.

"Mike was the pastor of a church in Beaumont, Texas at the time."

He also spoke about Michael's time in the Navy.

"Marla did not like Mike being away on detail for long periods of time, so she wanted Mike to get out of the Navy," the report says. "Mike was discharged from the Navy on June 20, 2002."

Garrison asked him about any problems the couple might have been having.

"Mr. Tabb stated that the only problem between Mike and Marla that he was aware of was that Marla did not like Mike drinking alcohol, even if it was just a little bit," Garrison reported. "Marla was devoted to her kids and her first duty in life was to take care of them. She would not think about getting a job as long as the children were young. She was a very strong-minded and independent lady. If a stranger came to the door, she would have opened it, even if she were in her pajamas. The front door was always kept locked by the deadbolt and people coming to visit would use the rear entrance to go in the house. Mike once told him they only use the front door to go out and get the newspaper."

Mr. Tabb acknowledged he hadn't spoken to his son that day; Michael had left by the time he had awakened from his nap.

CHAPTER XI

For God shall bring every work into judgment, with every secret thing, whether it be good, or whether it be evil.

Ecclesiastes 12:14

August 8-9, 2002

On August 8, Michael traveled to Beaumont, Texas – about a six-hour drive – for the visitation and funeral.

Tim Owen, Melanie's husband, had much to report to my detectives afterward.

Visitation began at 6 p.m. at the Kelley-Watkins Funeral Home. It's a grand building, all red bricks and white columns. There's stately marble and soothing music. It's the sort of place a preacher should feel right at home.

"When we arrived, Melanie's uncle told me that Mike had been by earlier and was coming back after he checked into the hotel," Tim explained later in a phone interview with Joe. "Melanie's dad and brothers were very upset and were concerned about what might happen when Mike returned. So I went outside and waited until Mike arrived with his dad, mom, brother and sister-in-law. I met Mike in the parking lot and told him that there was a lot of confusion, heartache, and speculation. I told him he needed to give Gene, Marla's father, a wide berth. He was completely non-emotional and said okay."

Mike then entered the funeral home, Tim said, which was filled with between 30 and 40 people.

"Everyone got silent," Tim reported. "Mike entered, walked around – talking to no-one – and looked briefly in the coffin. Then he came up to me and asked if we could talk. I said sure, and he and I went into a room by ourselves. The first thing Mike said was that he had come by the funeral home and asked about the payment for the funeral."

Marla's divorced parents, Gene and Sue, split the cost of the funeral.

"He said Marla was his wife and he was going to pay for the funeral," Tim said. "He said he would reimburse Sue and Gene. Which he has not done. He hasn't mentioned it again."

Joe waited for him to continue.

"Mike said he didn't kill Marla, but the police had already made up their minds and were not looking at anyone but him," Tim said. "He said they just wanted to close the case. He said the night the police interviewed him, they were friendly at first. Then, he said, they told him they had talked to the family and everyone thought he did it. So, he said, forget the family. I told him that was bullshit, and that we wanted him to be innocent."

Tim asked Mike who could have done this, "with so much overkill."

"He said he thought whoever did it must have panicked," Tim

recounted. "He said he didn't know anything, that the police hadn't told him anything. But he said he believed he would be charged. He said he would not spend the rest of his life in prison because he did not do it. I told him that Sue, Melanie, and I still hoped and prayed that he didn't do it, because the boys had already lost one parent and they didn't need to lose another. And again, he never asked about Sue or Melanie."

Michael Tabb then asked Tim if he should leave the funeral home.

"I said, 'Mike, we are all devastated, angry, and confused,' and that it might be the best thing," Tim reported. "He asked me if I thought he should go to the cemetery the next day, or just let it be a McCown thing. I said I did not think he should go. He left the room and went to his family and left about five minutes after that."

Throughout his few minutes at the funeral home, Tim says, Michael Tabb showed no sign of emotion or grief.

The funeral was no different, Tim reported later. The service was held at 10 a.m. on August 9, with the Rev. Jim Sliger officiating.

It began with an old Baptist favorite, C. Austin Miles' "In the Garden."

The first verse and chorus go like this:

I come to the garden alone

While the dew is still on the roses

And the voice I hear falling on my ear

The Son of God discloses.

And He walks with me, and He talks with me,

And He tells me I am His own;

And the joy we share as we tarry there,

None other has ever known.

There was a Scripture reading, Psalm 23, followed by a reading of Marla Tabb's obituary. After the singing of "Amazing Grace," another Baptist favorite, Rev. Sliger preached a brief sermon. The service ended with a prayer.

"Nothing was ever said to Mike or any of his family, by anyone else," Tim later told Joe. "We were so overcome with our grief that we were oblivious to him or his reactions during the service. But we heard about it from many of our relatives."

Reportedly, Michael Tabb was impassive throughout the service.

What happened later was unexpected. An even briefer graveside service was scheduled for 2 p.m. at the cemetery in Pineland, Texas, just east of the Houston area. It was about an hour-and-a-half drive, 82 miles away. The McCown family hadn't looked to see Michael or his parents there.

"Mike and his family arrived when it was about to start," Tim said. "He came up to me and said that he had to come, or he would regret it for the rest of his life. I told him that was fine, and I repeated that Sue wanted more than anything for him to be innocent, for the sake of the boys. And for the first time, he asked how the family was doing. I said, "Mike, they are crushed and devastated." He didn't say anything else and walked toward the service."

Mike didn't speak to anyone else during the ceremony.

"After it was over, Sue was talking to someone, and Mike saw her about three feet away from him," Tim said. "He got up quickly and walked away. He could not look at her. And he has never said anything to her. Mike and his family were the first people to leave. He never showed any emotion whatsoever."

Joe diligently typed up these conversations for future use.

CHAPTER XII

The words of a wise man's mouth are gracious…
Ecclesiastes 10:12

August 2012

I'd like to tell you more about Joe Rasco.

For one thing, he's even worse at retirement than I plan to be. He's retired from the U.S. Air Force, and he even retired from the sheriff's office – once. That didn't stick. But I'd better start at the beginning.

Joe was born in 1945 in Stamford, Texas, west of Fort Worth. His father was just returning from World War II, where he served in the U.S. Army Air Corps. He was the family's first child (he would later have three brothers and a baby sister). Joe's father re-entered the Air Force when the Korean War broke out in 1950, and remained in the service until he retired in 1974. Joe talks about their "nomadic" life as a military family. Joe lived in numerous states and countries as an "Air Force brat" – his words – until he graduated from high school, and went to college at Louisiana Tech University.

After graduating from LTU, he married his wife, Susan, who was also an Air Force brat. They'd been dating since she was 15 – their fathers were on assignment together at Barksdale Air Force Base in Shreveport, Louisiana. The two youngsters had lived one house away from each other.

When they were married, they lived everywhere from Kansas, Vietnam, Taiwan, Japan, Texas, Europe, Africa, the Middle East, India, Asia, Alabama, Delaware, and Arkansas. Joe was a tactical airlift pilot, driving the Lockheed C-130 Hercules ("Herk").

Joe describes it as "an adventure."

"Destinations few pilots ever see," he says. "The checkerboard approach into Hong Kong, the instrument landing system approach into Berlin, low-level tactical air deliveries and engine-running combat off-loads during the Khmer Rouge siege at Phnom Penh airport in Cambodia, stealthy CIA missions in unmarked planes – the gray birds."

Get him talking about his years in the service, and he'll tell you about flying behind the Iron Curtain into Romania, and you might even hear about some of the friends he lost. You'll hear about the other friends he made, the life-long friends. He'll talk about his multitude of "career-enhancing" jobs (we've all taken those, often to our regret – transportation officer, headquarters staff, squadron commander.)

"Those are all part of the business if you want to get promoted in the officer corps in the military," Joe says.

He taught "newbies" to fly the "Herk," and he trained endlessly. He worked his way up to lieutenant colonel.

After he retired from the Air Force in 1993, he looked around at his options for a new career.

"My choices included teaching school – I had a good background, having been in the military training game, driving an over-the-road truck, and law enforcement," he says.

He tried teaching, as a substitute, at first.

"Four months later, after having substituted in everything from fourth grade to high school, I decided you couldn't pay me enough to endure the torture," he admits. "My admiration for the teaching profession grew exponentially."

Yes, Joe is the kind of down-home Texan who uses words like "exponentially." It's one of the reasons I like him.

Next he tried truck driving – something that appealed to him because of all his years of nearly endless travel.

"There were good times and bad times," he says. "I hauled peanuts from Portales, New Mexico, Dell computers to Los Angeles, cheese to Pennsylvania, paper from Minnesota to Lakeland, Florida," he says. "I saw sunrises and sunsets to remember, and sat through traffic jams I'd rather forget."

While Joe loved the life, his wife, Susan, hated the time they spent apart. Joe agreed to try once more – this time, he would try his hand at law enforcement.

I have a policy – nearly everyone starts in the jail. That's where Joe started, doing his job well. After five months, he attended the East Texas Police Academy at Kilgore College. It's a 16-week program, and he was soon on the streets as one of my patrol deputies.

"That's where you learn the game – the criminal lifestyle," Joe says. "It was exhilarating and exciting, and even sometimes scary on the night shift – because that's when the criminals are out."

In my department, we're always on the lookout for talent. A good officer can advance quickly. Soon Joe was brought into the CID – the Criminal Investigation Division. He began by investigating property crimes.

"It seems brutally endless," Joe says. "But it's important. This is how those in the dope culture make their living – burglary and theft."

He also investigated white collar crime.

"That's an unappreciated venue," he says. "It's the least desirable case load among detectives, but it's quickly becoming the quintessential crime – the risk of getting caught is relatively low, and it takes a lot less effort than kicking in doors."

He moved on to personal crimes.

"Those are the crimes committed by the morass of basically hapless, dysfunctional people who constantly turn to violence to solve their issues, no matter how menial," he says.

Yes, that's Joe: "morass," "hapless," "menial."

"Desperation and anger, drugs and alcohol, contribute to probably 95 percent of such cases, and once you've seen the first 20, you've pretty much seen them all," he says. "Usually, murder is just an exaggerated extension of those acts."

Homicide investigation is the top of the law enforcement pyramid. Only the best make it in homicide.

"My first murder was in early 1998," Joe recalls. "A 15-year-old juvenile beat his neighbor to death with a tire iron – over dope, of course."

As part of my CID, Joe has helped investigate dozens of homicides since then. There's a common theme, he says: "broken lives, broken hearts, and broken families."

He doesn't do the investigations alone, of course. Just as Joe is Pam's mentor, Detective Noel Martin has been Joe's mentor. Martin has led the department in modernization and technological advances to make it one of the premier CSI units in the state (and I won't bother to spell out what CSI means – you already know).

As part of that effort, Joe has become our in-house expert on blood spatter – that's spatter, not splatter. We'll talk more about blood later, because blood proved to be the key evidence in the Marla Tabb case.

As a side note, my confidence in Joe is unsurpassed. In August 2009, I put together a Cold Case Unit. The detectives call it "homicide special." There are now 23 unsolved homicides on our books, dating back to the 1970s. I put Joe in charge of this unit. And that decision paid off. In May 2011, Thomas Lennon Dunn pleaded guilty to the deaths of Catherine Powell, a mother of two, in 1984, and of Frances Willingham, who had just been remarried, in 1984. The crimes occurred in rural Smith County.

Dunn was originally tried and given the death penalty in Mrs. Willingham's murder; that case was overturned on appeal, and never retried due to lack of evidence. But Joe was able to find DNA evidence in Mrs. Powell's sexual assault kit; based on that evidence linking Dunn to that murder. When Dunn was being interviewed about the Powell case, he confessed to Mrs. Willingham's murder, as well.

"It's interesting to note that during the cold case investigations, Dunn was serving a 25-year sentence for the random, at-knife-point sexual assault of Terri Pennington, which occurred 12 days before he killed Mrs. Willingham," Joe says. "Three of Mrs. Pennington's children were at home at the time of the attack. Dunn was driving the same car seen at the Willingham scene. It's inexplicable why Terri Pennington is not dead, like Catherine Powell and Frances Willingham."

He describes those cases as the work of a "stalker and a serial killer."

For years, I drove by the small wood-frame house where the Powell murder took place. I can still picture the crime scene in my mind today, and I'm glad that DNA and other developments were able to bring this case to a close. I can't speak highly enough of my team of detectives, and of Joe Rasco's persistence.

Joe tried to get away from me once; his "retirement" lasted from April to November of 2007 – about nine months. He came back in December 2007, and been with me ever since.

When he's not working for me, Joe is a golfer, a motorcycle enthusiast (he and Susan have matching Harley-Davidsons), and even a kayaker. As of this writing, he has three grandchildren. One of them, a granddaughter, wants to be a cop, he says.

CHAPTER XIII

The heart of the wise is in the house of mourning...
Ecclesiastes 7:4

August 2002

On August 13, my detectives started a second round of interviews. Those are always necessary, but never easy.

Pam was first; along with another detective, she went to our Children's Advocacy Center to try to interview the two-year-old son of Michael and Marla Tabb. He had been with his father, according to Michael, all afternoon on the day of the murder.

One note about the CAC — it's one of the places I helped found on behalf of victims in East Texas (I also co-founded the East Texas Crisis Center). It's hard for child abuse victims to travel from one agency to another, disclosing what they know about events in their lives. We established the CAC as a place for children to come and talk to all of the proper agency representatives in one location. Representatives from my office, Child Protective Services, Texas Department of Protective and Regulatory Services, Tyler Police Department, Smith County District Attorney's Office, the medical community, the mental health field and volunteers comprise the Children's Advocacy team.

The environment is non-threatening, friendly and calming. It's a place, we hope, where healing can begin. When I think about the two children left without a mother, I wonder about healing. I wonder if those children know — or if they will ever know — why their mother is gone.

That Tabb toddler was in a common room, playing with toys, when Pam approached him. He gave her his attention — but could

170

offer little more.

"He was just too young," Pam says. "He had a limited vocabulary, and he couldn't really talk about anything except the immediate."

That interview proved fruitless; her next interview would be more productive.

At about 2 p.m., Pam and Joe both rolled into the driveway of June and Lloyd Tabb. They had been interviewed before, on the night of the murder, but not by Pam and Joe. By now, the shock and disbelief had worn off. They seemed saddened now, even bewildered, but they were unwavering in their support for their son.

"Did they have any problems in their marriage?" Joe asked, when the pair had been led into the Tabb's living room. June had offered coffee.

"Some," June answered. "But that was a long time ago. Since they moved to Troup, things had gotten much better."

"How so?" Pam asked.

"They seemed happy," June replied.

"But not about everything," Joe prompted.

"No," June admitted. "Not everything. I know Marla had a housing issue with the church, but that's been resolved, I believe."

"Was Marla upset over the issue?" Joe asked.

"Yes. But Marla is… was… dramatic. She tended to exaggerate everything. That's probably how it was with Michael's drinking. I don't think it was as bad as she made out."

Joe changed the subject. "How was your relationship with Marla?"

"Good. We didn't see her much, mostly because of the military assignments. But my relationship with her was good."

Lloyd Tabb spoke up, volunteering information. "Michael and I were at the house in Troup today. We looked at the locks. The front door and the mud room door don't lock well. Michael also told me a wooden jewelry box was missing from Marla's vanity."

That caused Joe to pause. No one had mentioned a jewelry box before; he glanced at Pam. He saw in her eyes that she remembered the jewelry left out in the open in the bedroom.

"What was in the box?" Joe asked.

"I don't know," Lloyd replied. "He just said it was missing from her vanity."

"You think this could be a burglary?" Joe asked.

"I know Marla didn't feel safe in that neighborhood," Lloyd said, cautiously.

Remember, folks, the Tabb's home was across the street from the Troup Police Department. Joe and Pam both wondered what kind of neighborhood, exactly, could feel safer.

"She told Michael she would like to learn to shoot his gun," Lloyd added.

"He has a gun?" Pam asked.

"It's with his brother," Lloyd said.

"Tell us about Monday," Joe said.

That's how the interview went for a few more minutes, until Lloyd Tabb mentioned two curious facts.

"Michael told me he left the truck running when he went inside," Lloyd said as he related what Michael had told him about the day in question. But a few moments later, he added, "Michael said he was shaking so much when he went outside (of the residence) he couldn't get the key in the ignition."

The technical term for that is "a clue." All of the accounts agree; after finding Marla's body, Michael walked across the alley to a neighbor's house. He never said he attempted to drive anywhere; he never even said he stopped to turn off his vehicle.

"This is why you repeatedly interview subjects," Joe says. "These are the little inconsistencies that tend to come up. This is how you build a case."

But it's not like the movies; it's not even like the detective novels. That one glaring error in Michael's story might have been enough for a famous silver-screen sleuth to put away the murderer, but this is the real world. That means slowly and conscientiously building the best case we possibly can.

It means, for example, following that jewelry box rabbit-trail. A good defense attorney could take the absence of that box – in fact, the absence of evidence – and make it look to a jury like evidence of a client's innocence. Chasing that box would probably be a waste of time, the detectives knew. But not chasing it could be a fatal error in the investigation. The very next day, Pam was on the phone to Marla's mother again.

"Did Marla have a wooden jewelry box?" Pam asked.

"Yes," Sue McCown replied, after a pause. "But it's here."

"You have it?"

"It's been here in my house since they moved to North Carolina," Mrs. McCown said. "Marla didn't want to take it to the base. I don't think she trusted the on-base housing."

"And that's the only jewelry box she owned?" Pam asked.

"Yes," Mrs. McCown said. "The only one."

CHAPTER XIV

For in much wisdom is much grief: and he that increaseth knowledge increaseth sorrow.

Ecclesiastes 1:18

August 2002

"Blood will tell" is more than a proverb; it's a fact of criminology.

The blood was irrefutable evidence in this case.

You'll recall that even as detectives confiscated Michael Tabb's shoes, they noticed blood in improbable places. And you'll remember the blood spatter patterns in the Tabbs' bedroom, observed by my blood spatter expert, Joe Rasco.

I'd like to let him talk about blood, to explain its characteristics and its importance to this case.

He began forming his impressions when he walked into the room, he says.

"The first thing I noticed, other than Marla's body, was the blood spatter on the ceiling," he says. "That was very typical of when you use a blunt force object, particularly a large one. When you're hitting somebody over and over, well… after the first time you hit them, that blood adheres to that object, and when you draw that object back to hit them again, the blood comes off that object simply because of gravity and inertia."

You're "slinging" blood around the room.

"You raise the object again, as if to swing again, and the blood will come off coming down," he explains. "And you can delineate which are the forward strokes and which are the backward strokes, and in a lot of cases, you can tell how many times she was hit."

It's worth noting that while Joe saw clear evidence of blunt force trauma, and even had a good idea of how often Marla Tabb was hit – and even from where – an experienced assistant district attorney, Jim Huggler, couldn't even tell whether it was a bludgeoning or a shotgun wound. Joe's an expert.

"Sure, a shotgun blast is what it could look like, if you don't know what to look for," Joe says. "The scene would look fairly similar – because of massive injuries. But a shotgun simply doesn't do that."

A gunshot wound has a different blood spatter effect, Joe explains.

"When you shoot someone with a firearm, you don't get 'cast off' blood spatter," he says. "You get what they call 'high velocity' blood spatter. That's because of the impact of the bullet or that shotgun blast. It vaporizes the blood. It becomes a fog or a mist; it's not solid blood. That's how you start differentiating between what may have been used and what wasn't used. And there was no doubt when I saw that blood spatter on the ceiling that he hit

179

her with something. Did I know what he used? Well, no, I didn't. But I was beginning to have some idea."

Another indication was what crime scene investigators call a "void."

"During the attack, the blood is coming back and hitting him," Joe explains. If he's standing there above the victim, and he has a long object, then his feet are going to be spread out for leverage. You're going to have a void in that area where the blood spatter is not going to be, because his pants and his legs were there — and that's what we looked for."

That's why they immediately knew Michael Tabb's clothing and shoes would be very important during this investigation.

Joe also saw blood spatter on the walls of the couple's bedroom. This was a different kind of spatter; it was "impact" spatter.

"Once the victim is hit, the blood starts flowing," he says. "It's like taking your hand and slapping a puddle of water – smack, it goes everywhere. And it leaves a certain pattern on the wall, because it goes up in a high arc and then it hits the wall, and you can tell if it's impact spatter, high velocity spatter or cast off."

The wall spatter gave Joe a pretty good idea of where the killer stood.

"You can tell a lot just by looking at the blood," Joe says. "It's not an exact science like fingerprints, it's a discipline. It's like a polygraph. You can tell a lot about what happened at that crime scene by the blood spatter, and you use that information when you're interviewing somebody. If their story doesn't match what the blood spatter tells you, you know they're lying."

So far, nothing Michael Tabb had said was inconsistent with the story told by the blood; what was curious to my detectives, however, was Tabb's assertion, in the original 911 call, that it appeared Marla had been beaten to death with something like a baseball bat. He was right, of course, but that wasn't evident even to an assistant district attorney. That's a matter they would address later.

Other investigators handled Michael Tabb's shoes, and his truck. But Joe and Pam noticed something interesting about the truck, before it was hauled away to be examined, inch-by-inch.

There was a clean spot on it.

When Det. Noel Martin had the truck in our covered garage, he very carefully scrutinized and swabbed that curious clean spot.

Now, this is Texas, and it was August. There's dust. Any car or truck that isn't washed daily develops a film of dust. That film was uniform throughout the bed of Michael Tabb's blue Chevy pickup – except for one area, about a foot wide and about four feet long. Det. Martin found a sticky substance; a field test indicated it was blood. He sent it off to the Texas Department of Public Safety lab in Garland (about 90 miles west of here), along with Michael Tabb's shoes.

As detectives awaited the results of those tests, Joe and Pam say they knew it was important evidence.

"Evidence-wise, the Tabb case was a dream," Joe says. "That's the kind of evidence you're hoping for."

What he means is, once those results come back, you're just about done. In Pam's words, "you can't fight science."

It took more than a week for the initial tests to come back from the DPS lab in Garland. When they did, they indicated the substance was, indeed, blood. Based on that result, the lab said, it would do a DNA test to confirm that it was Marla's blood.

"There's absolutely no reason for Marla's blood to be in the bed of the pickup," Joe says. "What we think happened was he put the murder weapon, and the clothes he was wearing, in the truck. The 'swipe' pattern is a result of him dragging them back out, probably to dispose of them."

That simple act left blood, but took away dust. And that was enough. Michael Tabb thought he was covering his tracks; he was really just providing some pretty conclusive evidence.

It's the same with his shoes. They were oddly clean, in all the wrong places. And he missed traces of blood, and – forgive me – brain matter that the DPS lab later found in the laces and in the uppers.

As I've indicated before, his clothes were never found. Nor was the murder weapon. But as smart as Michael Tabb was, he couldn't completely hide the evidence.

Blood, as we've seen, will tell.

CHAPTER XV

And moreover I saw under the sun the place of judgment,
that wickedness was there; and the place of righteousness,
that iniquity was there.
Ecclesiastes 3:16

August 2002

On Tuesday, August 13, 2002, my top staff and I held our daily meeting. The No. 1 issue was Michael Tabb. We had been careful; even though he had stopped talking and asked for an attorney, we had refrained from calling him a "suspect." We didn't even refer to him as a "person of interest." But throughout the week following the murder, more than a dozen of my investigators were working hard to put together a case.

"Are we ready to get a warrant?" I asked, as we sat in the hot conference room on the fifth floor of the Carlton Building, an old hotel the county had bought and should have torn down years ago. The air conditioners weren't very convincing and the place leaked whenever it rained.

"I believe so," said Det. Tony Dana, who was the head of the department then. "Joe?"

Joe Rasco nodded.

"Get it written up and take it to the judge," I said.

And that's what Joe did. Here's what the Voluntary Arrest Affidavit says (and "the affiant" means Joe):

My name is Joe Rasco and I have good reason to believe and do believe that on or about the 5th day of August 2002, Michael David Tabb did then and there commit the offense of murder (felony) in that he did then and there:

186

Intentionally and knowingly cause the death of an individual, Marla McCown Tabb, by striking her with a blunt object unknown to the affiant.

My beliefs are based upon the following facts and information:

Affiant, Joe Rasco, is employed by the Smith County Sheriff's Department as a detective and as such is a peace officer in and for the state of Texas.

Affiant states on August 5, 2002, Smith County Sheriff's Department communications center received a call from a female who stated her neighbor was at the caller's residence and his wife was dead. A person who identified himself as Michael Tabb then got on the phone and stated he had come home to find his wife, Marla Tabb, deceased in the bedroom. Tabb stated to the dispatcher that the front door to the residence was ajar, and that his wife had been beaten, he added that it looked like with a baseball bat. The Tabb residence is located on S. Virginia Street, Troup, Smith County, Texas. Affiant knows that deputies with the Smith County Sheriff's Office were dispatched to that location.

Affiant knows that Smith County Sheriff's Deputy Mark Stinecipher was the first responder from that agency. Stinecipher informed Affiant that he responded to the scene and determined that Marla Tabb was deceased, confirmed by personnel from East Texas Medical Center EMS service. Stinecipher, with the assistance of officers from Troup Police Department, secured the house as a crime scene.

Affiant arrived at the Tabb residence and observed the body of a white female in the master bedroom next to the bed; she had sustained injuries to her head consistent with blunt force trauma. These injuries included several wounds to her face. Affiant knows that the lower portion of her face indicated multiple breaks to her jaw. There was no evidence of a forced, entry; valuables, including jewelry, were in plain view in the bedroom, and the home did not appear to have been ransacked.

Affiant knows that Det. Cecil Cox has spoken with Dr. Camp, a pathologist at the Southwestern Institute of Forensic Sciences in Dallas, Texas, who performed the autopsy on Marla Tabb. Dr. Camp stated that there were multiple injuries to her head that are between a blunt force trauma and a sharp force trauma.

Camp also stated to Cox that there was evidence of strangulation. Camp stated that Tabb had extensive injuries to her face including multiple fractures.

Based on the nature of the scene and discussions with Crime Scene Detectives Cecil Cox and Noel Martin, it was determined the perpetrator of the crime would have a significant amount of blood spatter on their shoes and clothing. Affiant knows that Det. Cox is trained in blood stain pattern analysis. Det. Cox has informed Affiant that there would be a large amount of blood spatter on the perpetrator of the crime. This is based on Cox's training and experience and the amount of blood spatter present in the bedroom, which indicates a void where the perpetrator would have been standing at the time of the commission of the offense.

During the investigation, detectives learned, from interviewing Michael Tabb and family members of Marla Tabb that the Tabbs had a history of marital problems including verbal and physical altercations; they had been married approximately four years and had lived in Troup about two months.

Affiant knows from interviewing Michael Tabb with other members of the East Texas Violent Crimes Task Force that he went into the master bedroom where he found Marla Tabb, knelt beside her, touched her arm, determined she was deceased, and immediately left the room. Tabb indicated he picked up his newborn baby from a playpen in the living room, went to his truck, got his two-year-old child out of the vehicle, and proceeded directly to a neighbor's residence to call 911. Tabb stated that he went to the Olive Garden in Tyler at approximately 11:30 a.m. He stated he left that restaurant and went to Broadway Square Mall because he did not find the people he was going to meet. He stated that he went back to the Methodist Church in Troup, then back to his residence, arriving at the residence at approximately 2:30 p.m. He then left the residence with his two-year-old son to go to his parents house at approximately 3:00 and made two stops before returning home at about 5:30. Affiant knows that Tabb's parents have been interviewed by law enforcement who confirmed that Tabb and his son arrived at their house in Tyler at approximately 4:00 and left an hour later. Tabb stated that he and his family had moved to Troup within the last two months and had previously lived in North Carolina where he was a chaplain.

Evidence collection included Michael Tabb's clothing, which was analyzed by Crime Scene Detective Cecil Cox. Detective Cox located a substance on Tabb's shoes; a presumptive test of the substance indicated it was in fact blood. Subsequent blood stain analysis of the shoes by Detective Cox and Crime Scene Detective Noel Martin led both, based on their training and experience, to believe the blood on Tabb's shoes was not consistent with patterns associated with simply walking into the crime scene or rendering aid. Specifically, the presumptive text indicated the presence of blood between the sole and the upper leather of the shoe, and in and under the laces of the shoes. Also, there was more blood on the left shoe than the right. This blood was not apparent without the use of forensic tests which is consistent with the shoes having been cleaned.

On Aug. 6, 2002, Detective Cox processed Michael Tabb's truck and located what appeared to be blood on the vehicle; a presumptive test confirmed the substance was in fact blood. This blood was located in the bed of the truck and covered an area of approximately one foot by four feet. This blood was detected through the use of forensic tests and was not visible to the naked eye. This would be consistent with that portion of the bed having been cleaned. Cox stated that this was consistent with a swipe pattern which indicated blood transferred from a bloody object(s) on a clean surface and pulled or moved over the clean surface. The bed of the truck appeared to have been wiped or cleaned in that portion, while the remainder of the bed was dusty with spots of dirt stuck to the bed.

Affiant knows from speaking with Det. Cox that in the carport of the house, Det. Cox located a square wooden table with two legs on, two legs off, one leg was laying beside the table, the other leg has not been located at this time. Cox stated there was a dirt track consistent with another table leg laying in the floor of the carport. Cox informed Dr. Camp of this, and the shape of the other table legs, and Dr. Camp stated that it could be consistent with the object causing the force trauma injuries to Marla Tabb.

Affiant knows that a pair of shoes has been collected from

Phyllis Cottle. Cottle was present in the residence prior to the arrival of the Smith County Sheriff's Office. Cottle went into the bedroom twice, close to the body of a Marla Tabb and left the residence. Her shoes have been analyzed by Detective Cox who found that no blood transferred to her shoes. This analysis was done by visual means and the same forensic chemical tests used on Michael Tabb's shoes.

On August 14, Detective Martin contacted the Department of Public Safety laboratory in Garland, Texas where a sample of blood taken from Michael Tabb's truck was submitted for analysis. There is an insufficient amount of blood to perform a test to determine if the sample is human blood, although there should be a sufficient amount of blood to enable the lab to develop a DNA profile."

Judge Diane DeVasto of the 241st District Court received the affidavit and issued the arrest warrant for Michael Tabb.

"The forgoing affidavit having been presented to me, and upon consideration of the facts and circumstances contained therein, it is hereby determined that probable cause exists to warrant the further detention of the above named accused," she wrote.

Since the day after the murder, the Smith County District Attorney's Office had been in contact with Tabb's lawyer, the inestimable F.R. "Buck" Files. Buck is just about the best in town. He's also an old friend. I knew he would fulfill his role. Late in the day on Wednesday, August 14, he escorted his client from his office, on the T.B. Butler Fountain Plaza (we just call it "the square"), across Broadway Avenue to the Smith County Courthouse.

Here's the *Tyler Morning Telegraph's* account of the arrest:

A Methodist minister suspected of bludgeoning his wife to death in the church parsonage almost two weeks ago was arrested Wednesday and charged with murder.

The Rev. Mike Tabb, 41, flanked by his attorney, surrendered to investigators at the Smith County Sheriff's Office after an arrest warrant was issued for the killing of his wife, Marla Tabb, 35.

Paperwork was processed, fingerprints made and the clergyman-turned-prisoner was whisked across the street to the courthouse, where he was arraigned by Judge Diane DeVasto in the 241st District Court.

He was released a short time later with no stipulated conditions, records show.

Jaws clenched, a grim-faced Tabb flanked by sheriff's investigators said nothing to the waiting gauntlet of reporters and photographers standing outside the courthouse moments before his arraignment.

Attorney F.R. "Buck" Files Jr. brushed off questions, saying, "This is a pending case. I don't comment on pending cases."

Inside the courtroom, the suspect – clad in a dark suit and still wearing his wedding ring – stood quietly beside his attorney, hired within hours of his wife's murder.

Assistant Smith County District Attorney Jim Huggler requested a bond of $50,000.

"We concur," Files said. "He has ties to the community, his parents are here in the courtroom. They have a homestead worth two times that, and they are prepared to post bond."

The case will be forwarded to a Smith County grand jury for possible indictment.

Sheriff's officials expressed confidence in the continuing investigation.

"We have taken our time and gathered a lot of forensic evidence," said Sheriff J.B. Smith. "There is plenty of it."

The Tyler Paper's reporter, Jacque Hilburn, uncovered some more interesting information about the Tabbs. That information was included in the article about Michael Tabb's arrest.

Events inside the Tabb household were not always peaceful, friends and authorities said.

Authorities, after interviewing family and friends, indicated the couple had a troubled relationship, dotted with instances of verbal and physical altercations, records show.

Friends described Mrs. Tabb as a bubbly woman with boundless energy, who was often the highlight of ministerial and civic activities.

She was an attentive mother, lavishing affection on her young sons.

But her perky demeanor was a sharp contrast to the shy, often withdrawn demeanor exhibited by her husband, friends said.

He tended to the children, but often appeared distant and detached emotionally to them and his wife, others said.

Still others described him as exhibiting signs of depression. "I often joked to her that I couldn't believe they were married," said Joyce Bays, a close friend of the victim. "They were very, very different – total opposites."

The couple was not well known in Troup, having moved to the area about two months ago following Tabb's discharge after four years in the military.

But they were very well known among military personnel stationed at Camp Lejeune, N.C., where Tabb served as a Navy chaplain, friends said.

Mrs. Tabb taught Sunday school at the base and was an active participant in the Japanese ministry, military personnel said.

On the surface, the couple seemed to have it all – good looks, a solid future, a strong spiritual base. At the time of Mrs. Tabb's death, they were the parents of two boys, ages 2 and 6 weeks.

Their marriage, like many, was not immune from trouble.

About one year ago, the couple lost a child to miscarriage. They were devastated, friends said, and began trying again to conceive.

Mrs. Tabb quickly became pregnant again, but suffered extreme bouts of morning sickness and other afflictions.

It was during the last days of her pregnancy that Ms. Tabb began reaching out to military friends, confiding darkly that she felt troubled by recent events in her marriage, friends said.

Prior to giving birth, the family suddenly announced to friends they were leaving the Navy, something never mentioned before.

Days later, they were gone.

Authorities said Tabb's discharge was honorable.

Tabb was hired by First United Methodist Church and they moved to Troup, settling into the church parsonage located one block from the police department.

Neighbors said the family led a low-profile existence. Mr. Tabb was often busy with church activities. Ms. Tabb was outdoors infrequently, but was always friendly to others.

On the night of her murder, neighbors frantically tried to comfort the couple's infant son, who had always been breast-fed and steadfastly refused to accept a bottle.

Authorities said neither child was injured during their mother's slaying.

Friends of the couple remain numb over the killing and unfolding criminal investigation.

Donna Sliger knew Mrs. Tabb from her high school days in Beaumont, where she attended Woodland Baptist Church and sang with a music group "Shining Light."

"Marla was larger than life," Sliger recalled. "She loved it and embraced it. But most of all, as was so very evident to everyone, she loved and lived for the Lord."

Mrs. Tabb's friend Terri Stock echoed the comments: "She always had a smile on her face and a song in her heart or on her lips. No one, especially Marla, deserved to die that way."

Michael Tabb bonded out of jail on $50,000 bail (put up by his parents). That's a relatively low amount, especially for a murder charge. It caused some grumbling in the community.

"Although he is innocent until proven guilty, this is a man of the cloth who has been accused of murdering his wife," one church member told the press. "A $50,000 bond is almost an insult to the community. It's been said he was a pillar of the community, but he has been here a very short time."

Another Tyler Paper article, published two days after the arrest, reflects the mood of the small community of Troup.

Shadowed initially by a cloud of public pity - now turned scrutiny - the minister has since been relieved of his spiritual responsibilities to the shell-shocked Troup church congregation.

Publicly, church affiliates said the minister is taking a leave of absence to get his personal affairs in order.

But those more familiar with the relationship between church and minister say the parting of the two is far more permanent.

Family members this week were observed removing items and personal effects from the church parsonage.

On Wednesday, the grim-faced minister walked out of the Smith County Jail a free man, at least temporarily. His parents attended his arraignment hearing and posted a $50,000 bond to secure his release.

Flanked by his attorney F.R. "Buck" Files, Jr., the minister, still wearing his wedding ring, was whisked in and out of the courthouse without public comment.

Although free, life for the widower will not return to normal.

The couple's two sons, ages 2 and 6 weeks, are living in separate residences. One with relatives, the other with a church member, officials said.

Authorities acknowledge the scope of their investigation has intensified and extends beyond Smith County.

We're going to see just how far outside Smith County the investigation went.

CHAPTER XVI

Suffer not thy mouth to cause thy flesh to sin...
Ecclesiastes 5:6

August 2002

Just as a clearer picture of Michael Tabb was emerging, a clearer picture of Marla Tabb was emerging, as well. On August 19 – two weeks after the murder – Joe went to visit Dr. Charla Spencer, the ob-gyn Marla saw when she arrived in Texas. Dr. Spencer was very forthcoming about the couple – both Marla and Michael had come to several appointments at her office.

The picture she and her staff painted of the couple was disturbing.

"The doctor indicated she witnessed Marla belittling Michael and calling him names while at the office," Joe's report reads.

He also spoke to Nancy Wilson, Dr. Spencer's financial officer, who dealt with the Tabbs on insurance matters.

"Mrs. Wilson also told me while in her office, Marla was belittling Michael so badly, she had to leave the room, because she was so embarrassed," Joe reports.

He left voluntary statement forms for them to fill out; he retrieved them a few days later.

"Marla and Michael Tabb were my patients for the last several weeks of her pregnancy," Dr. Spencer's hand-written statement reads. "They came to several appointments together and Marla came to two appointments by herself. Marla was very outspoken regarding her displeasure regarding their move to Troup. She was displeased with what she considered to be inhospitality from church members. She thought the town and the church wanted to control the way she lived her life and ran her home."

She had very pointed criticism of church members, and for the care that had been taken of the church parsonage.

"She was very proud of her voice talents," Dr. Spencer continued. "Michael was always very conciliating in his dealings with our office and was also very apologetic regarding her behavior during her c-section. He made sure to try to make all of the health care professionals caring for Marla know that she was very 'high strung' and we were not at fault for her anxiety during surgery."

The doctor noted that Marla had undergone a full physical exam in her first visit upon arrival in Texas, and another on the day of her caesarian section.

"She had no evidence of gynecological abuse," Dr. Spencer noted. "She did not have the demeanor of a typical abused woman that we see. She was not afraid to demean and humiliate her husband in public."

She added that her office had spoken to Michael Tabb on the morning of the day Marla was murdered – August 5. They confirmed an appointment for Marla on Tuesday, August 6, and faxed some insurance forms to the church office.

Mrs. Wilson, Dr. Spencer's financial officer, also submitted a voluntary statement.

"I had a lengthy conversation with Marla Tabb while Mike Tabb was present in my office," she wrote. "Marla Tabb was demanding, loud, and talked over her husband… verbally abusive to her husband to an extreme… unhappy with having been in the service (military)… unhappy with new living arrangements. I was embarrassed, left my office, and told my other coworkers how she was treating her husband. I could feel he was embarrassed by her actions, as well."

Later in the day on August 19, Joe and Pam spoke with Phyllis Cottle again. Mrs. Cottle is the wife of Gene Cottle, owner of the local funeral home. But she was also very active in the Methodist Church.

She told Joe she saw Marla as "immature and demanding."

"At least I don't have to live with her," Mrs. Cottle remembered thinking to herself. She added, "I can't find anyone who has anything nice to say about Marla Tabb."

Marla made at least one friend in Troup, however.

Phyllis McMakin gave a statement to Pam. She had met Michael, Marla and their son at a church service in June, at Walnut Grove United Methodist Church near Whitehouse, Texas.

"Marla and I became instant friends," Ms. McMakin said. "She had beautiful eyes and a beautiful voice, and I knew she had much training and talent in music."

She offered to help Marla unpack boxes (something no pregnant woman wants to do alone).

"On Thursday night, June 20, I called Marla and told her I'd be at her house on Friday to help her," Ms. McMakin said. "She started crying and said I was the answer to her prayer, that her mother, who was supposed to come Friday after work had just called and said she would not be there until Sunday afternoon late. Marla had hoped that she would help her unpack all the boxes."

Marla's baby was due just days later.

"I went to the Tabbs' at approximately 10 a.m. on June 21 and stayed there, unpacking, until approximately 7 p.m.," she says.

"During this time, Marla discussed many details of her life: her commitment to God and mission work, her hopes for Troup and Walnut Grove UMC to have mission work as first priorities. She discussed her early life and her parents' divorce when she was 15. She discussed her mother's depression and low self-esteem since their divorce – how her mother no longer attended church. She talked of her grandmother's death and pieces of furniture and things her grandmother had given her. She discussed how people in Japan had taught her to use baskets for storage. She showed me wedding pictures and baby pictures."

The boxes were stacked throughout the house, Ms. McMakin said.

The garage was so full of boxes you could hardly get in the door," she said. "I asked Marla if the movers were coming back. She said no, and she was certainly glad they were gone. She said one of those guys was a total creep – he made her skin crawl and looked at her funny. She believed he had a criminal record."

That's an important detail – could this be another suspect? The moving company, hired by the U.S. Navy, would certainly have extensive records on the move. My detectives would soon be digging into those.

"She repeated this at least once more during the day," Ms. Mc-Makin said. "She seemed very upset by this person."

Marla also aired some of her complaints about her new home and Michael's new job.

"We discussed the treatment she felt was very negative by the Troup church leaders," Ms. McMakin said. "She had bought white paint to paint the parsonage walls and they had said no. I saw the (wall) paper in the kitchen breakfast area that had been torn and taped. She said she had started to take it off before she was forced to sign a paper for the church committee saying she would not make any changes. She asked me if I thought that was fair. I said no, I thought the parsonage was her home."

That touched a nerve in Marla; this was going to be her "first real home," she told her new friend.

"She and Mike had kept many items in storage as they had been in Hawaii, Japan and North Carolina," Ms. McMakin said. "She said this was the first time she had unpacked her blue-and-white plate collection, at least 50 plates with various designs, and she looked forward to having them against white walls, instead of against dirty tan walls."

Marla also said that "three or four" families had keys to the parsonage, and had demanded to inspect the house "at random." She told Ms. McMakin, "they can just come in on me at any time."

"Marla kept saying she didn't know why she was telling me all this," Ms. McMakin continued. "She said it was upsetting to Mike and she might get him fired, that the district superintendent had already been called down on them by the Troup church, because of her wanting to paint."

Ms. McMakin described a loving family.

"Marla was very sweet and Mike worked hard unpacking boxes and hanging pictures," she said. "Their son would wrap his arms around Mike's leg when he was up on the stepladder and say 'Da-Da.' He was also hanging onto his dad everywhere he went. In the p.m., his dad put him in the car seat and rode him around in the truck until he went to sleep."

Phyllis McMakin's own husband came over in the evening,

bringing screws for the baby bed, screws Marla said the movers had "lost." Her husband and Michael Tabb made two trips to a hardware store to get the right screws.

"Mike was very attentive to Marla and kind to her and patient with their son," Ms. McMakin said. "I saw a very loving family life there."

Another picture of Marla emerges from an unlikely source – emails from Michael to the outgoing pastor of the church about the parsonage. It seems that from the start, it was a sore point for Marla. As early as March 27 of 2002, Michael Tabb was sending emails asking about the house.

"I wonder if I could impose on you for a favor," he wrote to the outgoing pastor. "In our phone conversation, you mentioned that you owned a digital camera and would be willing to take photos of the parsonage so that we could get an idea of the layout. My wife Marla would really appreciate it, as it would help her get an idea on how she is going to furnish the house. "

He noted that while most parsonages came with appliances, if not furniture, they had their own washer and dryer, and would need to sell them if they wouldn't be needed.

The outgoing pastor took photos, loaded them on a diskette (come on, it was 2002), and added a floor plan to the envelope when he mailed it.

But his note back to Michael Tabb indicates the parsonage was in good shape, and even undergoing some renovations.

"On the front of the house, they are terracing the front yard with new retaining walls," he wrote. "It already looks super nice! I'll send a picture when it's finished."

They exchanged emails about what children might live nearby (potential playmates for the children) and the names of pediatricians in the area.

An email dated May 1, 2002 indicates the two had a telephone conversation that seems to have left the other pastor disturbed.

"I wanted to be sure you understood what I meant about the carpet," he wrote to Tabb. "I don't want to tell you that you shouldn't ask for it, who knows? You may get it. I just wanted to say how much they have done in the last six years and that their willingness to do (improvements) for the parsonage family is not a matter of their attitude, it's a matter of their finances. They have made updates and renovations as they have been able to. On another note, the trustees are planning to have the outside painted, too. The front wall has taken longer than (expected), so I don't know about the timing of the outside painting."

Michael Tabb's brief response was, "I think that Marla has an idea about a color for the front. If they are planning to paint it before we get there, please let me know. Thanks again for your help."

A couple of days later, Michael was asking for more information – but making it clear that it was at the urging of Marla.

"Would it be possible to send us measurements of how much space exists between a wall and a window or door of rooms?" he asked. "This would help Marla as she plans where our furniture will go. If I'm asking too much, please forgive the intrusion and tell me that you don't have time. I'll understand. Regarding the parsonage committee's feeling that they have already spent a lot of money on the house, I do understand that sentiment. But I am willing to speak with them personally to plead our case, if that would help. Marla is really picky about some things, and quite frankly, I can't change that part of her! We are both looking forward to Troup and being back in Texas, and I'm just trying to do all I can to make sure she is happy with our home."

Michael apparently did "plead his case," and the outgoing pastor seems to have felt uncomfortable about how it was going.

"(The chairman of the committee) gave me a copy of your email about redecorating the parsonage, and I'm going to step out of all the discussions concerning the parsonage," he wrote. "We are very busy with bringing our ministry to a close, ending the school year, Little League, church choir, and getting ready to move to Van (Texas). We hope and pray for your best success here in Troup."

There's one more person's impression of the Tabbs I want to share. Beth Byrd, a retiree, was active in First United Methodist Church of Troup, and on its parsonage committee. She first spoke to Michael Tabb on March 16, 2002, when the district superintendent told them that Michael had been assigned to the church.

Now, if you're a Methodist, you probably already know that pastors are assigned to churches. The United Methodist Church's own website explains it this way:

"Rather than local churches hiring and firing their own pastors – as in some denominations – United Methodist bishops appoint pastors to serve in local churches and other ministry settings. One advantage to this process is that a local church never has to go without a pastor… The primary goal of the appointment system is to match the gifts and graces of a particular pastor to the ministry needs of a particular congregation at a particular time."

As a member of the Parish Relations Committee, Mrs. Byrd was given a "biographical sketch" Tabb had prepared for church members. She called him to welcome him.

"It was a cordial conversation," Mrs. Byrd told Joe in a voluntary statement. "I told him I would send a copy of the pictorial directory of the church, along with budget information."

She did so, she said, and Marla sent a nice thank-you note. Mrs. Byrd also learned of their son's second birthday (from the biographical sketch) and sent a gift. Marla replied with another thank-you note, along with a photo of the child opening the gift.

Mrs. Byrd sent more information and material to the Tabbs.

"My next contact with Mike was June 4, when I called him at his parents' house in Tyler, from the parsonage in Troup, around 5 p.m.," she said. "I told him we would be shampooing the carpet around 6 p.m. Mike and Marla had asked for and expected the carpet to be cleaned professionally by Steamatic. He indicated in the conversation that he and Marla would be out later in the evening. I left the parsonage around 6 p.m. and went home. Around 8 p.m., it is my understanding that Mike and Marla did arrive at the parsonage, where there were about 20 people working – painting, cleaning the carpet, polishing shelves, etc. I was not there when they arrived, but it is my understanding that Marla was upset and disappointed that she was not going to get to paint, wallpaper, etc. as she had requested by email. Marla was very verbal about her dissatisfaction. Others will have to tell you what was said and done, since I know only what I have been told."

Mrs. Byrd says perhaps Marla's discomfort (she was eight months pregnant, after all) was a factor. Mrs. Byrd wonders why she would even be moving halfway across the country when her pregnancy was so advanced.

"Why not assign an interim minister to Troup so Marla would not have to change doctors at this critical time for her?" Mrs. Byrd asked. "(That would) give her sufficient time to recover from the birth and then move to Troup. Parishioners questioned the wisdom of the move."

I'm sure those parishioners meant well, but I can see how Marla might see them as, well, busybodies. But Mrs. Byrd continued her statement.

"From Tuesday night until Thursday (June 6), parishioners (were) most unhappy with Tuesday night's events," she said. "They were considering asking the Tabbs not to unpack, to keep on moving. The situation continued to boil."

Michael Tabb seems to have sensed the seriousness of the situation caused by his wife's behavior.

"On Thursday, in the late afternoon, Mike called me to set up a meeting to try to clarify the situation," Mrs. Byrd said. "I told him the chairman of the Pastor/Parish Relations Committee was the one to call the meeting. If he called a meeting, I would certainly attend."

But then Marla attempted to intervene.

"About an hour after Mike called, Marla called in tears, begging to meet with me, since I was the only one she knew by name. I told her I would be glad to meet with her and listen to her side of the story. I met Marla at the church on Thursday evening and talked with her for about two and a half hours. She went into great detail about her background and explained why she had submitted a 'list of demands.' She had not intended for the list to be considered demands, but what she preferred, if possible, to make the house seem like her home. She wanted to paint the rooms different colors, wanted the wallpaper in her kitchen to match the blue-and-white dishes. She said she and Mike had spent $200 on paint and they stretched their budget to do so. She talked about her Southern Baptist denomination to quite an extent. She told about her miscarriage, her difficult time at her son's birth. She would have a c-section with her second, and she did not intend to do anything for six weeks so she would not experience the pain and infection she had with her first. She related stories of their several moves because of problems with the houses. She talked about her allergies and her son's, to clarify why she was so particular about having the carpets professionally cleaned. She related her many accomplishments through the years and she felt sure she could make a contribution to this church after recovery from childbirth."

Marla told Mrs. Byrd she worried her behavior Tuesday night would hurt Michael's career.

"I told her it was the custom for ministers to move into the parsonage without comment, assuming, of course, that the house was in good condition," Mrs. Byrd said. "After a parsonage family has been in the house for a while, the parsonage committee would respond to their requests for changes. However, I doubted she could do the painting she wanted because it had been freshly painted in neutral colors. She could feel free to use colors to decorate the rooms with curtains and wall hangings. She continued to insist this was to be her home for a while and she should be allowed to paint the walls, as long as she agreed to repaint them before she vacated the house. I was firm in my statement to her that I seriously doubted she would be allowed to paint the walls."

She said that during the lengthy conversation, Marla never mentioned marital problems.

"She did say they had to be careful about their finances," she said. "She wanted to know what she should do to mend fences and ask for forgiveness for her behavior. I suggested that she relate much of her story to the people involved in a meeting on Friday night. She asked if I thought these people would forgive her but continue to hold it against her. I told her I really could not answer that, but we had to start somewhere."

Michael entered the room at that point, Mrs. Byrd said.

"On Friday night, Mike and Marla met with the parish members, most of whom had been at the parsonage on Tuesday night," she said. "Mike related his ministry work and his accomplishments. Marla then read her statement. She referred repeatedly to her Southern Baptist upbringing."

Folks, that's a no-no. Just in case you hadn't figured that out from Mrs. Byrd's tone.

"Once again, she asked to be allowed to paint the walls her colors," she said. "Once again, she was told no. She was again told she could decorate in drapes and wall hangings and whatever way she wished. She was told the kitchen wallpaper would be changed in a couple of months, after she recovered from childbirth. This meeting concluded amicably."

But Marla seemed unable to let go of the matter. The next day (Saturday, June 8), Michael met with Mrs. Byrd at the parsonage, as Mrs. Byrd was overseeing the cleaning of the home's air ducts. The two spoke for a few minutes.

"Again, Mike asked if I thought they would be allowed to paint," she said. "I told him no, not after what he had been told on Friday night."

On Sunday, Michael Tabb preached his first worship service at Troup United Methodist Church. He introduced his family, but he seemed nervous. Mrs. Byrd's account of the service would be comical, if it didn't indicate real problems. Change is never easy, and the Tabbs weren't making it any easier for either themselves or their new parishioners.

Mrs. Byrd explained that Michael Tabb didn't seem to be sensitive to the moods of his new congregation.

"He did not conclude the service until after 12:20 p.m.," Mrs. Byrd said. "Although the congregation was irritated by such a long service, they were lenient in their words because it was Mike's first Sunday. The church honored the Tabbs with a reception during the afternoon. They were presented with generous gifts from the church. The reception went well. At various times, Marla made mention of her Southern Baptist membership, which did not go over too well with the Methodists."

During the following week, the Tabbs were focused on moving. Michael only stopped by the church office to drop off books. According to Mrs. Byrd, they asked that new dead-bolt locks be put on the doors. Those new locks were, in fact, installed.

Mrs. Byrd describes some of the adjustments she asked Michael Tabb to make – sticking around to visit with members after the sermon, for example, and wearing a lapel microphone.

"Mike seemed very uncomfortable in the pulpit, awkward with the worship bulletin," she said. "I told him he could change the order of worship if it would make him more comfortable. He appeared to be 'running scared,' lacking in confidence. He had trouble following the order of worship; he mostly read his sermon."

She was also critical of his pastoral ministry skills.

"I made several offers to go with Mike to visit shut-ins and other members of the congregation," she said. "He never responded, and he made no visits. It seemed someone had to tell him the next step to take."

Mrs. Byrd was at the hospital when Marla had her c-section on June 25. She also visited Marla when she and the baby were discharged.

"I went to the parsonage to the mud room door and rang the doorbell," she said. "Marla came to the door and unlocked it."

Mrs. Byrd underlined "unlocked."

"The doors were always locked," she said.

"On June 30, I talked with Mike about his office hours," she continued. "In three weeks he had been in the office less than two hours. I advised him he needed to come to the office a minimum of four hours a day, four days each week, at the same time the church secretary was there. I reminded him that he was the supervisor of the secretary, the janitor, the lawn care people and the music people. I asked him specifically to meet with the choir director to coordinate the music for worship (he never did this). Mike said he would be in the office the next day. From this point on, he came to the office, but he often brought the 2-year-old son with him, complicating the flow of work for him and the secretary."

Mrs. Byrd had lots of other advice for Michael.

"I also told him at this time he should learn about the financial reports and how to prepare them," she said. "I subsequently gave him a list of what was needed for the finance committee on July 9. The secretary prepared the material by herself. Mike was silent during the meeting."

Mrs. Byrd went on to list a few other complaints about Michael Tabb, such as being unprepared for meetings.

But there's one incident that sticks out.

"During the (Administrative Council) meeting, his only comments were about his dissatisfaction with the Lakeview camp for the young people," she said. "Even though he had not been associated with Lakeview for a number of years, he expressed concern (about) teenagers' sexual activity while at camp. The comments were inappropriate in this setting."

On Sunday, August 4 – the day before Marla Tabb's murder – Michael seemed "preoccupied," according to Mrs. Byrd.

"He read an unusual sermon at Troup about homosexuality, which drew unfavorable comments," she said.

She noted, after the service, that a key to a file cabinet, where they kept the offering, was missing. Michael said he had taken it home. He returned it, "without comment," she added.

"In summary, Mike was ill-at-ease in the Troup church," Mrs. Byrd said. "He and Marla isolated themselves, and the congregation could not get to know them. They kept the house totally locked, and on more than one occasion, members of the congregation who brought food to them were not invited in. The food was taken at the door. In my opinion, the congregation at Troup did all it could to welcome Mike and Marla, but they projected the feeling they did not want to be a part of the Troup church."

There was one more thing Mrs. Byrd shared with Joe, verbally. She told him she knew all of the church members – well – and that there was no one, as far as she knew, who was angry enough to harm Marla Tabb, for any reason.

Many of Mrs. Byrd's complaints about the Tabbs would be echoed by other church members, and soon by some of Michael's military superiors.

Later, I talked to both Gene and Phyllis Cottle. You'll recall they're the funeral home owners and church members who had lots of contact with the Tabbs, and were personally involved on the night of the murder. How? Both Phyllis and Gene were some of the first people on the scene, after the police arrived. They saw the body and talked with Tabb; Tabb went home with Phyllis (just a few blocks away) so that he could borrow some of Gene's clothes when my detectives asked for his, as evidence.

Gene and Phyllis also took Marla's body to Dallas for the autopsy, later that night.

But their first impression of the Tabb family, weeks before, was much like Mrs. Byrd's.

"We're Methodists, so we're used to pastors coming and going," Gene says.

So the church was excited, but not necessarily surprised, that a new pastor with a young family was being sent to serve them.

"The preceding pastor had been there for seven years or so, and it was probably about time for him to move on and move up," Gene says. "I've been a member since 1977 – the church dates back to 1864 – so we've seen a lot of pastors come and go. The church carries on."

During the summer of 2002, Gene served on the Pastor-Parish Relations committee. He was one of the church faithful who cleaned the parsonage and fixed it up, in preparation of the Tabb family's arrival. He and Phyllis were inside the house, in fact, with Gene painting baseboards and Phyllis cleaning the carpet, when the Tabbs dropped by prior to moving in. They heard a commotion outside, and Gene was called out to talk with Marla. She was upset that professionals weren't in there, doing the work.

Now, you have to understand the nature of the Cottles' business. They're funeral directors. They're used to meeting very stringent health codes, and making everything perfect for somber ceremonies. Is there anything a professional house cleaner could do that Phyllis Cottle hadn't already done? Not likely.

Phyllis shook her head. "I don't think they really need to even unpack that truck," she said.

But she didn't really mean that, Gene adds. They continued with their work, and when the Tabbs moved in, the house was as close to a home as they could make it.

"I understand what Marla was saying about things like the wall paint, and the carpet, and such," Gene says. "Everyone wants to make their house their own, in a way."

But this was a Methodist church parsonage – a house that different families would move into every couple of years, in most circumstances.

"We have to keep the colors neutral, it's as simple as that," Gene explains. "It's not a permanent home for anyone, really. It's not meant to be."

Whatever the cause – whether it was the wall colors or just the Tabbs' natures – their relationship with the church itself never recovered from those initial conflicts, the Cottles say.

"They were always stand-offish," Gene says. "Michael Tabb never really opened up to anyone."

The typical church service was a brief, uninspired sermon.

"Preaching and pulpit-ability aren't the most important things a pastor needs in this particular church," Gene says. "They're helpful, and we've had better preachers and worse than Mike Tabb, but he wasn't that hot of a speaker."

The thing is, he wasn't very good at the other parts of pastoring – visiting the sick and the shut-ins, counseling those with problems – either.

As other church members had said, Michael Tabb would show up right before the service was to start, and he left quickly afterward. He wouldn't stand around to greet church members, to shake hands, or mingle. Many church members took offense.

As for Marla, she was rarely there at all. Because Michael would also preach at nearby Walnut Grove Methodist Church, she would attend that one (when she attended at all).

"She ignored our church," Gene says. "I only remember seeing her here one Sunday — and she sat in the back. I don't think she stayed at all."

Like any church, members reached out to the new pastor's family, mostly with food. Casseroles arrived, but oddly, the Tabbs never asked people to come inside, even when they were bringing gifts of food, Gene recalls.

When people in the church were around the couple, they sensed tension.

"That's not something we see in hindsight," Gene says. "We felt it then, and we talked about it some. I know I felt sorry for him, even before it happened."

But in many ways, the Tabbs were a different couple in the eyes of the church members at Walnut Grove. That small congregation hadn't dealt with Tabbs' demands and scenes at the parsonage. When the murder occurred, "It caused something of a conflict between our two churches," Gene explains.

"They couldn't believe that Michael could have done anything like that," he explains. "Well, we had seen the strife and the problems and everything. There were a lot of folks in our congregation that could, to be honest."

On the night of the murder, the Cottles were at their home eating dinner. The phone rang, and a church member told them to get to the parsonage as quickly as they could.

"Forward the phones to the answering service and follow me," Phyllis told her husband as she rushed out the door.

When she arrived at the parsonage, three blocks away, Michael Tabb and a church member were standing in front of the house. Michael was quiet. A police officer asked Phyllis if she wanted to see the body; she answered that she would have to eventually, so she might as well.

"I said out loud, 'wow, somebody was mad,'" she recalls. "This wasn't just a robbery or even a rape. This was beyond that. The scene was horrible. And I see a lot of horrible."

Back outside, standing beside Tabb, she began to think about practical matters. She asked Tabb where the children were. He pointed down the alley.

"I went and there was the neighbor, with one child in her arms and one at her side," Phyllis says. "She said the baby was hungry and the other needed a diaper and she didn't know what to do; she didn't have anything like that. He had just dumped his children on her."

Phyllis took charge; she asked Tabb how the baby was fed – breast-fed or formula? Tabb responded that Marla used both.

"You know babies are particular about bottles and formula, so I asked the police officer if I could go see what she was using," Phyllis says. "He said I could. In the kitchen, I found a bottle in the sink; I took it with me, and I told him it had nothing to do with the murder, but I needed it to take care of the baby."

As she ran to the grocery store for supplies, she called another church member – who had children, and importantly, child seats for their car – to come by and take the children.

When she arrived back at the home, she handed off the children and again went to Tabb. She could see that her husband had arrived and was talking with officers.

"It was such a hot August evening," she recalls. "We had to get out of the heat. I took him to my Suburban and I turned it on, just for the air conditioning."

When a detective approached and asked for Tabb's clothing, it was Phyllis who suggested going to her house for a change. The detective agreed, and said he would follow.

Of course, Gene recalls that moment, too. He had been inside the home, too, and had seen the body.

"I also saw the jewelry," he says. "Already the story wasn't adding up for me. One of the detectives was near me, after I came out, and he said something about a search. I remember telling him I didn't believe he'd have to look very far. This wasn't a stranger killing, in my mind.

And that's when he saw his wife leaving, with Michael Tabb in her vehicle.

As Phyllis remembers, "We went in, and I found Tabb some jeans, a shirt, and some of my husband's old sneakers. The detective stayed in the bedroom with him while he changed."

When they emerged, the detective left. Tabb was alone with Phyllis and one other church member.

"He was very calm," she says. "He didn't say anything about either his wife or his children. We talked about books on my shelf, we talked about football. It's what he didn't say that bothered me, more than what he said. He never once asked who could have done this. He never asked why."

Gene adds, "That's what people usually ask, when a loved one has been killed. They want to know why. They want to know who."

The Cottles didn't get to discuss the murder between themselves until the next day, even though they drove the body to Dallas late on the night of the murder. On the way home, however, they began to compare notes.

For the church, the murder was traumatic, but not devastating.

"Honestly, they hadn't been here that long, and when they were here, they hadn't really formed any relationships," Gene says. "So I guess overall, the church held up well."

There was shock, of course, but it was limited. "We knew there were problems. But no, we couldn't have thought anything like this would happen – but we could see how it might," Gene says.

"We didn't blame ourselves," Gene adds. "We knew the problems began a long time before he ever arrived in Troup. They arrived with those problems."

There was some anger at the hierarchy of the Methodist Church; Phyllis explains that although there were warning signs – the conflicts over the parsonage, for example – the hierarchy never warned the church about the Tabbs. In fact, the church asked for a meeting with the state bishop a couple of weeks after the murder.

The hierarchy, you see, had asked the Troup church to pay for some of Tabb's accrued vacation time – as sort of a severance package. That horrified the Troup church (but not the Walnut Grove congregation, which was the source of further conflict between the two).

When the bishop arrived for the meeting with the Troup leadership, he listened patiently to all they had to say.

"When I was little," he reportedly responded, "My mother whipped me some. Enough to know I'd had a whipping. Well, I guess I've had one now."

One person who helped ease the trauma for the church in Troup was Rev. George Heldon. He was a retired Methodist pastor, who had actually been at the Troup church about 20 years before. Retired now, he stepped in as an interim pastor. He knew many of the families and was trusted by all.

"He really was the glue that held us together," Gene says.

Nowadays, no one at the church really talks about the murder of Marla Tabb.

"Methodist churches aren't really tied to the person, the personality of the pastor, as much as some denominations," Gene explains. "That's just how we are. Like I said before, the church goes on."

CHAPTER XVI

*Wisdom strengtheneth the wise more
than ten mighty men which are in the city.*
Ecclesiastes 7:19

August and September 2002

Late August and September were busy for my Criminal Inves-

tigative Division. Pam and Joe continued to chase leads and talk

to potential witnesses. They checked out Michael Tabb's story; on

August 23, for example, Joe timed the drive that Tabb told investigators he made on the day of Marla's murder. He found that it took 22 minutes to drive from the Tabb's home, in Troup, to his parents' home in Tyler (with a brief stop at the Brookshire's in Troup); it took another 12 minutes to reach the Brookshire's in Whitehouse; and then another 13 minutes to return to the Tabb home.

They would compare this to Tabb's story.

Joe and Pam obtained a list of everyone who was at the Tabb's home – when it was still the empty parsonage – on June 4, when Marla had reportedly made a scene. They spoke to everyone; they collected more statements.

Pam was able to confirm that in fact, the Methodist ministers did have an informal luncheon planned for the first Monday of each month; however, the group's plan for August 5 wasn't to meet at the Olive Garden – it was to meet at Posado's Mexican Café.

"The way I look at it, this is just part of the business," Joe says. "There are the exciting parts of it – the interviews with suspects, walking into a crime scene for the first time, seeing a judge sentence a bad guy. This isn't the exciting part. It's the mundane part."

Joe keeps a good perspective on all the leg work, which is crucial to building a tight case, but it can be boring as hell.

"It's like flying airplanes," says this veteran combat pilot. "Sometimes you can fly an airplane, especially a tactical airplane, at low levels, yank and bank, but when you're up there on a cross country with navigator in training, and you're just sitting there on auto pilot, it's the same feeling. We're slowly and steadily gathering facts and statements, going down the road looking for evidence. It's just that mundane stuff."

But that "mundane" part of the job, if performed poorly, is what lets criminals walk. Joe and Pam know this; that's why they're so thorough.

Take the moving company, for example. What do some movers, hired by the Navy to transport the Tabbs' worldly goods from North Carolina to Texas, have to do with Marla's murder more than two months later?

You'd be surprised.

For one thing, both Pam and Joe have made cross-country (and for Joe, even overseas) moves, courtesy of the United States military. As a Navy man myself, I know the military is obsessive about paperwork.

Take that curious three-legged table that Joe first noticed in the Tabb's carport.

"The military thing in me was setting off alarms," Joe says. "Maybe that table leg was missing when the family moved. That's possible. But if it was, you know good and well the movers who contracted with the Navy would have noted that on the inventory. The government is pretty firm about things like that. No moving company is going to take responsibility for a three-legged table without making a note of it first."

Joe's first move was to call officials at Tabb's base in North Carolina. He made contact with a Navy Criminal Investigation Services officer (yes, NCIS), an agency he would soon be working more closely with. He obtained the name of the moving company and requested an inventory of the move. It was J.A. Haralson Moving & Storage of Tyler. He gave them a call.

Joe notes in his report from August 27, "received copy of household goods inventory from Tabb move from North Carolina to Troup; inventory does not reflect a table leg missing from any table."

And remember Phyllis McMakin's statement, which said that Marla felt one of the movers was "creepy" and made her nervous? That had to be checked out, too.

That's just the kind of small loose thread a good defense attorney can tug, in court, to make a whole case unravel.

He might ask, "Did you bother to look into Mrs. Tabb's fears? No? Why not? Was your focus solely on Michael Tabb? Did you investigate anyone else? Or was your mind made up from Day One?"

I've seen it happen. That's why my detectives have to be so thorough.

On September 17, Joe and Pam went to Haralson Moving to talk to the owners. They learned there were three movers who brought the Tabbs' goods to their new home: two men, and one woman. They further learned that on the day of the murder, both the men were working at Haralson's site until 7 p.m. And the woman? Well, she was in my jail that day. Cross them off the list.

Another pertinent fact emerged from my detectives' contact with the moving company.

"In discussion with Haralson and some of his employees, detective (that's Joe, remember) learned when the Tabbs' household goods were delivered, Marla Tabb called the moving company 14 times, expressing her displeasure with the move-in," Joe wrote in his report. "The moving company was forced to contact the Traffic Management office at the Dallas Naval Air Station three times, due to Tabb's complaints."

CHAPTER XVII

So I returned, and considered all the oppressions that are done under the sun: and behold the tears of such as were oppressed, and they had no comforter...
Ecclesiastes 4:1

August and September 2002

As soon as Pam and Joe began to learn more about Michael Tabb, they realized sex was going to be an issue in this case. There was the story about Marla finding a listing of escort services in

Michael's pocket when they were in North Carolina.

Michael's excuse was that he'd taken the list from a young Marine he was counseling. Marla didn't seem to believe him.

"I was on one of the calls where Melanie (Marla's sister) brought that up," Joe says. "Up until that point, I don't think it ever crossed my mind that something like that was going on. But after that conversation with her, we began to wonder."

"We were running everything through our minds, as we do, looking for motive," explains Pam. "We don't always find out what the motive is – which bugs the crap out of us – but when we're looking for that, we have to consider everything."

There were other indications that something was wrong - those were also mentioned by Melanie during telephone interviews.

Michael's unexplained absences, for example. He would disappear for a weekend or even longer; he wouldn't be able to account for money he spent, or what he was doing. He said he went to motels to drink.

"That could be," Joe says. "But other things happen at motels, too."

There was another odd fact - something that didn't quite fit. Michael's final sermon at the First United Methodist Church in Troup was about homosexuality. It made more than just Mrs. Byrd uncomfortable; Gene Cottle mentioned it, as well.

"Members of the church were taken aback by the subject matter," Cottle told Joe. "We thought it was an inappropriate subject for a new preacher that didn't know the congregation well."

When Pam and Joe searched the home, they came across some literature from a group called "Transforming Congregations," based in California. It's a group, founded by a Methodist pastor in Bakersfield, dedicated to "transforming" homosexuals into heterosexuals. It's a controversial topic and a controversial group (though in 2002, it had a bit more acceptance).

Cottle reported that one Sunday, Michael Tabb had put copies of the brochure in the church bulletin, and put more materials on a table outside the church office.

"Transforming Congregations is committed to provide (sic) information, resources and training to churches, districts and annual conferences in understanding and involvement in ministry of transformation of homosexuals, and also to encourage trans-forming ministry based on loving compassion, Scripture and the discipline of the United Methodist Church," the literature found in Tabb's home read.

Since then, the group has changed its focus some, but its website says it still wants to teach churches how to help the "sexually confused."

How?

Congregations can "challenge the myth that homosexuals cannot change," the literature says. "To believe that homosexuals cannot change is a great impediment to any homosexual's initiation of the healing process."

Churches can also "offer a warm and welcoming place for those struggling with homosexuality... Those who are successful in leaving homosexuality behind are those who find friends in a supportive congregation – people who understand their struggle and compassionately encourage them to succeed."

Folks, we're talking about a small-town, generally older (if not downright elderly) congregation. Homosexuality wasn't a burning concern for most members of First United Methodist Church of Troup.

Why did Michael Tabb gather this literature? Why did he preach that particular sermon?

"We may never know," Pam acknowledges.

Still, it was something to file away as something that just didn't fit.

As I've emphasized repeatedly (and with good reason), Joe Rasco spent a lifetime in the military. He knows there's temptation at every turn – there's not a military base, that I know of, that doesn't have adult-oriented bars or businesses just outside the gates.

That got him thinking; he and Pam were beginning to suspect that Michael Tabb was doing some catting around in North Carolina.

"We were trying to figure out why he was holing up in the hotels in North Carolina," Pam explains. "Was he having an affair? Was he seeing prostitutes? Was he just trying to get away from Marla? We really didn't get a solid answer, other than he liked to drink and he couldn't do it at home. But it was still a suspicion that we thought we should look into."

"People are creatures of habit," Joe says. "You learn that pretty quickly. I figured, well, if he was doing that in North Carolina, would he be doing it here?"

He shared this hunch with Pam; she agreed it was a good one. Together and separately, they began to check the motels in the area.

Pam learned in early September that Michael Tabb had checked into the Super 8 Motel. She saw his blue truck – since released from CID – in the parking lot, she told Joe. She watched him as he drove around that afternoon; she saw him coming away from the vicinity of the old Economy Inn.

"The Economy Inn is a known location for drug and prostitution activity," Joe noted in his report.

This was just over a month after his wife had been murdered.

Over the next few weeks, the detective kept following that hunch. In early October, Joe drove by Tabb's parents' home, and saw that his truck was not there. He then drove by that Super 8

Motel, and saw Tabb's Chevy pickup in the parking lot.

He began a stake-out. Tabb opened the door at 4 p.m. and again at 10 p.m., but he never left the room, nor did anyone else ever enter it. Joe stayed until 11 p.m. (it had been a long day already) but he was back by 5:30 a.m. the next morning.

"At 8:30, Tabb opened door but did not exit," Joe's report reads. "At 10 a.m., Tabb exited room and walked north on balcony to unknown location and returned alone in a short time. At 11 a.m., Tabb exited room and went to his truck and put unknown object in truck. At 11:30, Tabb exited room and went to Stratford (House Inn), next door to Super 8, and entered lobby."

Joe saw his chance. He called Det. Noel Martin, a top crime scene guy, and went to the front desk of the Super 8. He asked for, and was given, permission to search room 211, the room Tabb had just vacated.

With Martin at his side, Joe collected 29 empty cans of beer on the bathroom counter, an empty 30-pack box for the beer, an empty jar of dip and an empty pizza box.

Michael Tabb had been there for less than two days.

The very next day, my detectives had the same opportunity to search Tabb's room at the Stratford. This time, Pam was along for the fun.

While searching room 205, which Tabb had checked out of just a few minutes before, they took photos of "several empty chip bags, 12 empty beer bottles, an empty beer can (probably beer No. 30 from that 30-pack in the Super 8 room), an empty dip jar and a Hustler magazine under the mattress."

The clerk at the Stratford told them she'd seen Tabb dispose of a small cooler in a trash bin at the foot of the stairs, outside the room. Joe retrieved the cooler. It contained "a condom box, a partial bottle of mouthwash and a container of hair gel."

Later in the afternoon of October 4, Joe and Pam confirmed that Tabb was back at his parents' home in Tyler.

But the incident led them to broaden their inquiries. They phoned the motels and hotels in the area, and learned that on Friday, August 23 through Sunday, August 25, Tabb had stayed at the Tyler Sheraton – this was just 18 days after his wife had been murdered.

He paid with an American Express card – Pam notes that during the interview with Tabb on the night of the murder, Tabb claimed he had no credit cards.

During a follow-up call to the Stratford on October 9, Joe learned that Tabb had checked in again, just that morning. Joe drove to the motel to begin a stake-out.

Tabb remained in his room for most of the day, but at 5 p.m. he emerged and got into his truck. Joe followed him to the Time Out Club, a well-known (but rarely discussed) local strip club.

"I called Pam and said 'you aren't going to believe this,'" Joe recalls.

Joe also called for backup; as he waited outside, undercover officers went into the club and videotaped Tabb as he, well, enjoyed the view.

About two hours later, Tabb left the club – but he didn't return to the motel. Instead, he went to his parents' home. Once Joe was convinced he was there to stay, at least for the night, Joe returned to the motel.

"During the stake-out I noticed the suspect exit his room, go

to a trash can and deposit a pizza box and a red/white carton,"
Joe's report says. "I retrieved the items from the can and located
eleven 12-ounce Budweiser cans in a Budweiser carton, a single
16-ounce Budweiser can and a Pappa John's pizza box. Items
were photographed and the cans and carton were logged into
evidence."

Tabb didn't return that night, despite having paid for the room.
He did, however, return the next morning and pay for another
night, and also a third night.

Did he need to stay at a motel? His home was still a crime
scene, but he was apparently welcome in his parents' home. He
had a place to go, but he didn't go there much. That reinforced
my detectives' suspicions.

When Tabb checked out a few days later, Joe was ready to search
the room again. The maid admitted she had removed numerous
Budweiser cans from the trash receptacle Joe had searched before; still, there was a beer can in the room, along with two pizza
boxes, and something curious.

In Joe's report, he describes "what appeared to be blood/semen stained bed sheets." The can, and the sheets were logged into evidence.

Tabb returned to the Time Out Club on October 25. And on October 28, he was back at the Super 8 Motel.

Also in October, Det. Noel Martin completed his search of Michael Tabb's computer hard drive. That was a long time ago, and technology wasn't quite as advanced, but he was able to find a number of pornographic images saved on the computer. Seems Tabb had an affinity for porn star Christy Canyon; but compared to some things we find these days, the images seem pretty tame.

There were no images of males on the computer, that Det. Martin could find.

Of course, we've got this forensic software now that can go into a hard drive and find things that were deleted, files that were erased, and places the user had been. We can go into the registry. But back then, we just didn't have the technology for that.

What conclusions could my detectives draw from Tabb's activities? Unfortunately, nothing solid.

"Sometimes these kinds of things can convolute an investigation for us," Joe says. "You know they may be relevant, but then again they may be so far out there that they just put you on the wrong track. That's part of what we have to sort through."

These are rabbit trails you've got to follow.

"But in the end, there was no smoking gun in that computer, and no smoking gun in the motel rooms," Joe says now. "I don't see it as a waste of time. We were just doing our jobs."

I have my own opinion about the sexual aspect of this case. I'll express those later.

CHAPTER XVIII

Wisdom is better than weapons of war:
but one sinner destroyeth much good.
Ecclesiastes 9:18

September 2002

Joe came to me earlier in the investigation and said they would
need to travel to Camp Lejeune in North Carolina to delve deeper into Michael Tabb and his marriage to Marla. On September
25, he and Pam drove the 110 miles to Dallas-Fort Worth Inter-

national Airport for a flight to Jacksonville, North Carolina.

I knew they were right.

It's a six-hour flight from the grand Dallas-Fort Worth International Airport to the smaller facility outside Camp Lejeune. Pam and Joe drove together to DFW (about a two-hour ride), and then waited through the enhanced security in those days just a year after Sept. 11, 2001.

What did they talk about?

"What do we always talk about? The case," Pam responds. "We wear it out. We go over every detail. Again and again. That's how we work."

Their flight left DFW, bound for a connection in Charlotte on Thursday, Sept. 26, 2002. They arrived in Jacksonville in the afternoon; they rented a car and checked into their hotel rooms.

In the morning, they drove through the gates of Camp Lejeune, a huge, sprawling, 246-square-mile complex on the Carolina coast. Both being "military brats," they felt more at home than most of my detectives would have. In fact, there's a particular reason I made sure to send Joe on this assignment. It wasn't just his familiarity with the case.

They met with Special Agent Marine Sgt. John Eversole, a real-live NCIS detective. During the next two days, he would escort my two investigators as they interviewed Michael Tabb's superiors, his acquaintances, his friends and those he ministered to.

Sgt. Eversole was a relatively new investigator at that time, but he was a rising star. He would soon be assigned protection duties for some of the military's top brass.

Pam describes him as a real Marine – tall, no-nonsense, dedicated.

They began by briefing Eversole on the case when he picked them up at the front gate's waiting area, driving a black Buick.

"He was curious and attentive, but he didn't pry, and he didn't try to offer any opinions," Pam recalls now. "He was very professional."

The tall, dark-haired Eversole "facilitated" their interviews – and by that, I mean he made them happen. There were some folks who wouldn't have talked with Joe and Pam otherwise.

But early in the day, Pam carefully let drop one fact: Joe Rasco was a retired lieutenant colonel. You could almost see Eversole sit up straighter as he drove the dark, government-issue Buick around the sprawling base.

"I know Joe wouldn't have said anything himself," Pam says. "And that's just like him. He wouldn't have wanted to make anyone else uncomfortable. We weren't there in any kind of military capacity, so he probably wouldn't have thought it would be relevant. But the fact is it helped us out tremendously. A lot of doors opened to us, that wouldn't have opened to just ordinary civilians."

One thing my detectives would learn from the people at the base was that the Michael and Marla Tabb, who "just couldn't fit in" in Troup, faced the same difficulties at Camp Lejeune.

Their first interview was with the senior chaplain for the Second Marine Division. It took place in one of the many, many faceless gray buildings that seem to fill any military base. There was a steady flow of uniformed men and women, less chit-chat than you'd see in a civilian office building, and a deference to the civilians as they were being led to different offices. Joe carried himself with his usual self-assuredness. That's his natural state. Maybe that lent something to the air of deference they felt around them.

Pam had a little trouble keeping up with Sgt. Eversole's steady, long strides. But she sure wasn't going to say anything. From time to time he would notice, and slow down a bit.

When they were led into his small office, Capt. Donald Larow couldn't really offer much; he knew Michael Tabb but wasn't his direct supervisor.

"He was aware the Tabbs were having marital difficulties but did not know specifics, other than Marla Tabb had called various agencies on the base, including Michael Tabb's supervisor, and the Inspector General's office, complaining of Tabb's being deployed and insisting he be returned home," Joe's report reads. "He further indicated he was aware Tabb had some issues with alcohol and his work performance was substandard and he had been transferred several times (because of it)."

Capt. Larow told Joe that Tabb had taken a job at a church off the base, against military rules.

"He was extremely upset with Tabb for violating policy," Joe reported. "He (also) recalled that Tabb did not participate in various required meetings and functions."

Next, Pam and Joe spoke with Lt. Com. Larry Jones, who was Tabb's supervisor for about six months.

"He had no discussions with Tabb about job or activities while Tabb was stationed in Japan," Joe wrote. "Tabb was a 'closed person,' no in-depth conversations about family or personal issues. Tabb was unhappy with the Navy and wanted out."

Like Larow, Jones mentioned that Marla contacted Michael's supervisors to complain.

That's a career "kiss of death" in the military, Joe says now.

"I was a squadron commander," he says. "I know what I would have thought if one of my subordinate's spouse had called to yell at me."

In that interview, Jones also mentioned two instances in which Tabb failed to perform required duties, apparently because of Marla.

"He had verbally counseled Michael Tabb about job issues, and he was present when Marla Tabb called fellow officers, screaming over the phone, because Tabb had been directed to attend a function and spouse wanted him home," Joe's report reads. "He indicated she 'exploded.' He was also aware of her calling the Inspector General's office complaining about Tabb being deployed."

The next interview was with Dr. Susan Demchak, Marla's doctor at Camp Lejeune.

"She provided a written statement indicating Marla Tabb had become her patient in May 2001, had a miscarriage shortly thereafter, called Demchak's office in May 2002 in tears, stating spouse had left and taken car keys and leaving her stranded," Joe's report recounts. "She interviewed Marla Tabb at her office and (Marla) Tabb indicated it was the second time spouse had left her, gone to motels, spent money and drinking. Spouse called her a 'bitch.' (Marla) indicated spouse's brother had killed himself."

Even more information was gleaned from Dr. Demchak's receptionist. She vividly recalled the incident the doctor had mentioned; that day, Annette Metter drove to the Tabb home to pick up Marla and take her to the appointment. She recalled Marla being nearly "hysterical" and upset. But she refused Ms. Metter's offer to get her some help.

"She said when they moved to Texas, near her family, everything would be all right," Ms. Metter recalled.

She had only heard from Marla Tabb one more time, when Marla called from Troup to ask about her medical records.

Pam and Joe then interviewed Lt. Col. David Hough, commander of the First Battalion, 8th Marines. Tabb had been transferred to Hough's unit, despite "problems" in his job performance.

Hough said he hoped that the transfer would be a "fresh start for Tabb."

But Tabb wasn't there much, and wasn't doing his job, Hough said. In fact, many of his Marines had never met him, didn't know Michael Tabb was their chaplain.

He knew about Marla Tabb, of course – he knew she was a "screamer and a yeller."

Even after several months, Tabb never got around to moving into his new office.

"When Tabb should have been solving problems (for his men), he was creating them instead," Hough said.

There were more interviews; the consensus was the same: Michael and Marla Tabb had problems. Marla had trouble getting along with people; Michael had trouble handling her and even handling his job duties.

Joe believes that Michael started at a disadvantage at Camp Lejeune.

"You see, Marines don't have their own chaplains," he explains. "They have to use Navy chaplains. A Marine's attitude is that some people are Marines, and if you're not, you're not."

It didn't help that Michael Tabb was seen by those who knew him as "non-aggressive." One neighbor even used the word "wimp."

Marines are aggressive – that pretty much defines a Marine.

Michael Tabb didn't even act like a non-Marine chaplain. He wasn't close to his men; he didn't open up to them, or even spend time around them. He didn't spend time with his fellow officers, either, according to several of the interviews." He was passed over for promotion; his superiors knew about (but didn't address) his growing problem with alcohol. Although his superiors counseled him repeatedly, he was never formally disciplined. They simply viewed him as "trouble."

No one seemed sorry to have seen the Tabbs leave for Texas.

Pam and Joe also got more details about the incident when the Marine MPs were called out to a motel room; no one was arrested, but the MPs, a Sgt. Davis and Sgt. Hawks, noticed a large amount of alcohol in the motel room where they found Tabb. The incident was resolved peacefully (they left, after determining Tabb wasn't breaking any laws, and Marla came to take him home).

They also spoke to some neighbors, including one who had hosted the couple at a Christmas party the year before. The Tabbs had seemed happy, that young man said. But he said he felt little but surprise when he saw on the news that Marla had been murdered, and Michael was the main suspect.

"They just didn't respect him," Pam says of the people at Camp Lejeune. "That's what I came away with. Not his men, not his neighbors – we couldn't really find any friends – not his fellow officers. Maybe they just didn't know him. But they didn't respect him."

There's one more thing I want to tell you about that North Carolina trip. Joe's hunch about Michael Tabb frequenting, shall we say, adult-oriented businesses proved to be correct in Tyler. How about North Carolina?

Their second night in Jacksonville, Joe knocked on Pam's hotel room door. It was maybe 8 p.m.

"You up?" he asked.

Pam remembers groaning in response. If she was, it wasn't by choice.

"What do you need?" she asked.

He told her his plan (through the door). She reluctantly agreed.

And my two detectives, on county time and in a county-rented vehicle, proceeded to cruise the strip clubs that surround Camp Lejeune.

They visited four or five clubs, Joe reports, but turned up nothing. They assured me they didn't drink anything while in the clubs, and they didn't go at peak hours. They always identified themselves to the managers and dancers, and just showed a photo of Michael Tabb to see if anyone remembered him. No one did – or at least, would admit it.

Was Pam scandalized? She rolled her eyes when I asked.

"After everything I've seen?" she asked.

CHAPTER XIX

Then said I, Wisdom is better than strength: nevertheless the poor man's wisdom is despised, and his words are not heard.
Ecclesiastes 9:16

September 2002

Joe first noticed a disassembled, square wooden table in the carport on the night of the murder. Two legs were on, two were off. One leg was leaning next to the table. The other, well, just wasn't there. Dust patterns on the floor showed where it seemed to have been.

That night, my detectives took that loose table leg into evidence. It wasn't the murder weapon, but they were already starting to suspect it might be the mate of the murder weapon.

Joe's expertise in blood spatters led him to believe it could be; even Michael Tabb's inti al 911 call gave investigators an idea of what they should be looking for.

When he said his wife had been killed with something "like a baseball bat," he was "basically telling us what he killed her with," Pam says. "We knew what to look for."

It wasn't exactly a baseball bat – though one was later recovered from the home, discovered under a piece of furniture. But it was close.

The autopsy report provides the best evidence of this. The murder weapon had to be both blunt and sharp. It had to have the heft and swing of a bat, but with cutting edges that could cause the type of lacerations on Marla Tabb's head, neck and torso.

That describes the table leg exactly. Long, cylindrical, and squared off at the top – just like its mate – it would explain the injuries and the spatter.

What's more, it was a weapon of opportunity.

Michael Tabb could have been on his way out the door. He could have made it as far as the carport. His rage, boiling over and looking for any outlet, would have been uncontrollable. He could have seen the table leg – and seen a way out.

There's still some uncertainty about the exact time of Marla's death. But the probable timeline my detectives established would have Michael Tabb arriving home in the mid-afternoon. An argument could have escalated, culminating in the murder at roughly 3 to 3:30 p.m. That would have given him time to collect his wits, gather up what evidence he could, and leave the home. He would have had time to dispose of that evidence before he arrived at his parents' home in Tyler, at around 4 p.m.

The search for the missing table leg began on the night of the murder, as cops checked nearby bushes, yards, ditches and even a patch of woods down the street.

Nothing.

269

Later, more careful searching turned up nothing, as well. We began to expand the search. Joe and Pam reasoned that Michael Tabb said he'd travelled from Troup to Tyler on that day – and by now, we had the video evidence from the grocery store to prove it.

So why couldn't he have dumped the murder weapon, and perhaps his clothes, along the way?

That launched a search that eventually included dozens of officers from several different agencies, my mounted horse patrol, deputies on three-wheelers, and Pam Dunklin going dumpster-diving.

I wasn't there to see her digging through a dumpster in the back of a grocery store. I believe I'm glad of that.

On August 14, the day Michael Tabb surrendered for a voluntary arrest, deputies were combing through the buildings, bar ditches and trash cans along Texas Highway 110, all the way from Troup to Tyler.

The search lasted for days. At the end, Joe sums up the results in his report: "No hit."

It was, literally, looking for a stick in miles of woods.

"It was fruitless, and it was frustrating," Joe says. "But you've got to make the effort. That's what a lot of people don't understand too. I learned from an assistant district attorney, early on in my career, that when you go to a crime scene and do your investigation, you'd better be thinking about court."

You think about all the holes you'd better plug before a case goes before a jury or a grand jury.

"That's something Pam and I both have learned over the years," Joe says. "It's a slow process. The way you learn about your mistakes is to get on that stand, and have a defense attorney get in your business about what you didn't do. You learn real quickly."

If my detectives are ever unsure, I encourage them – no, I require them – to check with a supervisor or an assistant district attorney.

The day of the "Lone Ranger" is gone. That's just the fact. We cooperate. We pool resources. We can't depend on just one agency, or one person, anymore.

The search for the murder weapon was just that sort of cooperative effort. You've seen how busy Joe and Pam were; they couldn't devote the sheer number of man-hours it took to conduct that search properly.

And Joe's right; as I've said before, a defense attorney will look for any little weakness in a case – "Where is the murder weapon? Didn't you search for it?" They look for a crack and they'll make it a chasm.

My detectives were determined not to let that happen.

CHAPTER XX

I returned, and saw under the sun, that the race is not to the swift, nor the battle to the strong, neither yet bread to the wise, nor yet riches to men of understanding, nor yet favour to men of skill; but time and chance happeneth to them all.

Ecclesiastes 9:11

November 2002-September 2003

What closed this case? That's easy: the DNA evidence. All the hard work Joe and Pam put in, interviewing people, collecting evidence, checking stories and facts, helped build a strong case.

The DNA helped make an unsinkable case.

That's what juries want these days. They want that irrefutable proof – what they've seen on television. Maybe it's easier that way; maybe they don't have to make those tough decisions.

"And guess what?" Joe reminds me. "Unfortunately, a lot of the district attorney's offices are like that, now, too. With juries in this mind-set, it's really hard to get a conviction in a circumstantial case anymore. I'm not saying it's impossible, but they don't like circumstantial cases. It's a CSI world now."

That's why, when the DPS lab in Garland notified Joe on the morning of November 13 that the blood found in Michael Tabb's truck and on Michael Tabb's shoes was Marla Tabb's blood, he knew they would get a conviction.

Joe still had faith in the case they'd built; they established clear means, motive and opportunity.

"We also had the circumstantial evidence saying there was no way that blood could ever have gotten on top of those shoes," he adds. "I think maybe we could have gotten there – gotten to a conviction – without the DNA. But you know, when you throw the DNA on top of all that, it's just icing on the cake, baby. That's what it's all about."

The formal notice came in a letter dated November 9 (it took a few days to find its way to Tyler).

It was signed by DPS Criminologist R. Greg Hilbig. He was working with six specific samples.

"DNA typing was performed on selected samples using the polymerase chain reaction (PCR)," he wrote. "The DNA profiles from the stains from the right shoe of the suspect, the left shoe from the suspect, and the suspect's vehicle, are consistent with the DNA profile of the victim."

How "consistent" is "consistent?"

The scientific term is "pretty damn."

"The probability of selecting an unrelated person at random who could be the source of this profile is approximately 1 in 2.452 quadrillion for Caucasians, 1 in 1.381 quintillion for Blacks, and 1 in 15.94 quadrillion for Hispanics."

For the record, a quadrillion is one thousand million million, or

1,000,000,000,000,000.

"Based on these probabilities, the victim is the source of the stains from the right shoe from the suspect, the left shoe from the suspect, and the suspect's vehicle," Hilbig concludes.

"You can't explain that away," Joe says.

He's right. Michael Tabb – and his attorney, Buck Files – knew it, too.

Here, of course, my involvement pretty much ceased. My investigators were also done, for all intents and purposes. They kept in touch with the district attorney's office, but now, it was a lawyer thing. Buck Files and the Smith County District Attorney had to try to work out a plea agreement. If they couldn't, the case would go to trial.

The case continued to get publicity; a fairly accurate account of the case appeared on "Dateline NBC" on January 3, 2003. I was pleased with it. When that show was filming, I was feeling confident – maybe even a little cocky.

"That minister better start singing 'Amazing Grace,' because he's going to prison," I told the reporter.

But someone said the wheels of justice grind slowly. It was several more months before we heard anything about a plea agreement. In fact, Michael Tabb was nearing his trial date.

Then, in April 2003, Judge Diane DeVasto granted a continuance, just days before jury selection was supposed to begin.

District Attorney Jack Skeen Jr. wouldn't say much, but he told the press, "I cannot comment on the status of any plea negotiations in the murder case. We are continuing to prepare for trial."

I ain't dumb; I knew what that meant. We expected a plea agreement any day.

But then the final twist in this case came. I'll have to rely on contemporary press accounts for much of the information, because my department didn't handle it. We didn't even know about it, at first.

Our first indication something was wrong came on May 13, 2003, the day when Michael Tabb was supposed to plead guilty to the murder of Marla Tabb.

Joe Rasco was on his way to the courtroom – where Melanie Owen, Tim Owen, Sue McCown and several other friends and family members of Marla Tabb waited. Joe had gotten a call earlier from the district attorney; "Get down here – now."

"I thought to myself, oh crap," Joe says. "What's this going to be about?"

The district attorney wouldn't answer any questions. He just demanded Joe's presence. And he wasn't happy.

Pam wasn't in the line of fire that morning; she was at home, sick.

"I would have been there, if I could," she says now. "I was just sick as a dog. I would have been there for the show."

The "show," however, was mostly the judge glaring down at poor Joe Rasco. The clock was ticking. The district attorney was waiting. The judge was waiting. The family members were waiting.

Michael Tabb wasn't there. He was supposed to agree to a 50-year-sentence, in exchange for a guilty plea. This was going to be the only chance Marla Tabb's family would have to confront him.

They weren't happy. No one was.

The clunky ticking of the plain round clock could be heard over the hushed talk in the pew-like seats of the 241st District Court. The courtroom in the Smith County Courthouse was filled with staff from the district attorney's office, law enforcement officers, reporters, and most of all, family members of a young mother who was killed in her home almost a year before.

The defendant's chair sat empty.

Rasco could feel Judge DeVasto's eyes on him. The clock ticked past 9 a.m., the time when this hearing was supposed to begin. It was to be just a procedural hearing; the defendant's lawyer had negotiated a plea agreement and a 50-year sentence for his client. That client was now late for his hearing.

Judge DeVasto exhaled loudly enough for everyone in the quiet courtroom to hear. She looked straight at Rasco.

"Find him."

Rasco nodded, rose from his front-row seat, and strides to the door. He was out in the hallway when his cell phone rang. It was Pam. She didn't know how timely her news about the defendant would be.

Joe listened for a moment. He was almost – almost – at a loss for words.

"Shit."

Pam, prostrate on her couch at home, had learned of Tabb's whereabouts before Joe did.

"I was so mad because I couldn't be there in court," she says. "But a few minutes later, I get this phone call from my daughter, who's attending the University of Texas at Tyler. She says, 'Mom, you're not going to believe this…' She told me some guy had just tried to cut his own throat at UT."

Pam responded with concern, and her daughter offered this detail: "His name is Michael Tabb."

"I said, okay, call me back with the details and tell me that you're okay, you're safe," Pam says. "I called Joe and said my daughter just called me, and said there's some guy at UT that got his throat cut named Michael Tabb."

Joe rarely curses. This time, I think it's excusable.

"You've got to be shitting me," he said. Then he paused. "Well, he didn't show up for court this morning, so I guess that makes sense."

Here's a portion of the *Tyler Morning Telegraph's* account, published the following day:

A Methodist minister scheduled to plead guilty Tuesday to the murder of his wife is recovering under guard at a Tyler hospital after slashing his throat and tossing the weapon into a snake-infested pond.

Smith County District Attorney Jack Skeen Jr. confirmed Michael Tabb's neck wounds were self-inflicted. He said Tabb, 42, was to accept a 50-year prison term Tuesday morning for the beating death of Marla Tabb.

When help arrived, Tabb claimed he had been attacked... He had been living with his parents, whose home is close to The University of Texas at Tyler.

Emergency personnel were summoned around 9 a.m. to the campus off University Boulevard after a man with throat wounds was sighted lying beside the pond north of the library.

"Based on reports of the results from the police investigation, it certainly appears to be self-inflicted," Skeen said.

He said Tabb tossed the weapon into the nearby pond, which was reported to be swarming with water moccasins. Authorities said a witness saw Tabb hide behind a tree and flick a knife into the murky water.

"Officers are out there searching for the knife but water moccasins are everywhere, and they are slowing the search down," Skeen said.

He said Tabb was in the intensive care unit Tuesday afternoon at East Texas Medical Center and is expected to recover. He had been free on bond since his arrest last August for the beating death of Mrs. Tabb, 35, just weeks after she gave birth to their second son.

As a result of Tuesday's events, state District Judge Diane DeVasto raised Tabb's bond to $1 million and ordered he be transferred to county jail upon his release from the hospital.

About the same time as police were called Tuesday to the campus to begin their investigation, prosecutors and Tabb's attorney, Buck Files, were scratching their heads at the downtown county courthouse.

Tabb, on Files' advice, had agreed in the last several days to a plea bargain in which he would admit to bludgeoning Mrs. Tabb.

The former Troup minister left his parents' home around 8 a.m. Tuesday, advising he was going on a quick walk before attending his 9 a.m. court appearance.

Looking back, Pam, Joe and I all doubt Michael Tabb's sincerity in that suicide attempt.

"If you're going to kill yourself, you're going to stick a gun in your mouth," Joe says.

"Or swallow the whole bottle of pills," Pam adds. "But this knife business, that's just stupid."

The whole episode can be summed up pretty well with that word, "stupid." There was no reason for the Tyler Police Department, which took the call, to suspect that Michael Tabb was supposed to be in court, pleading guilty to murder. The story he gave the responding officers was that he'd been assaulted – robbed, even. By the time he was taken to the hospital, however, they had it figured out. They posted a police officer at his room, since he was a suspect, not a victim.

The next day, Tyler police went looking for that weapon.

Again, here's the *Tyler Morning Telegraph's* story:

Tyler police continued their search Wednesday for the knife Michael Tabb allegedly used to slash his throat just before he was scheduled to plead guilty to murdering his wife.

The former Methodist minister is recovering under guard at East Texas Medical Center.

Smith County District Attorney Jack Skeen Jr. confirmed Tabb's neck wounds were self-inflicted.

He said Tabb, 42, was to accept a 50-year prison term Tuesday in the death of Marla Tabb.

A detective and crime scene technicians searched the pond Wednesday from about 8 a.m. to 4 p.m., said Chris Moore, Tyler public information officer.

The officers used metal detectors and continued to drain the 3-foot-deep pond, which was taking longer than expected.

Moore said officers planned to continue their search for the weapon Thursday morning.

Tabb claimed he had been attacked when help arrived at The

University of Texas at Tyler, where he lay bleeding next to the pond north of the library. He had been living with his parents, whose home is close to the campus.

Emergency personnel were summoned around 9 a.m. Tuesday to University Boulevard.

Skeen said Tabb tossed the knife into the nearby pond. Authorities said a witness saw Tabb hide behind a tree and flick a knife into the murky water.

Tabb is expected to recover from the knife slashes to his neck.

The knife was recovered the next day.

I think it was desperation. He was desperate. His world and the life he had spent years building – through college, through seminary, through his years in the Navy – was about to end with the finality of a judge's gavel. At this point, all the education and religious counseling in the world can't lead you down the right path, because all this pressure is coming in on him. He knows he's going to spend what seems like the rest of his life in prison.

Most of the people we deal with are used to it; getting caught and getting sent to prison is just part of the game. But it was another world to Michael Tabb. It had to be frightening.

As the newspaper reported, Judge DeVasto increased Michael Tabb's bond to $1 million. He wasn't going anywhere. The district attorney took his offer of 50 years off the table and said he would take the case to trial.

Michael Tabb, however, had no stomach for that. And on September 29, 2003, he stood before Judge Cynthia Stevens Kent to plead guilty and accept a 55-year sentence.

(Judge DeVasto had been appointed to the 12th Court of Appeals three months before.)

First, he had to face the family of the woman he had so violently murdered.

"Did she suffer?" he was asked by Melanie Owen, Marla's sister. "You mutilated her so badly that we did not have the chance to look at her beautiful face one more time... The district attorney's office has pictures of you at a topless bar five days after you murdered Marla, and we won't go into evidence about your hotel visits."

She told him the family is "haunted by thoughts and images of

286

what you did to Marla."

She added that they wonder and worry that perhaps the 2-year-old watched his father "beat his mommy to a pulp."

Throughout their testimony, Michael Tabb said nothing. He just stared down.

Michael David Tabb will be eligible for parole 27 and a half years after his sentencing date. I wonder what he's doing now. Is he ministering to the prison population at the Texas Department of Criminal Justice? Or is he withdrawn, keeping to himself, much as he did before he went to prison?

My staff and I talk about this case.

We know it's changed us, maybe in ways we don't like.

Pam feels that she's grown harder.

"Maybe I used to think that some people couldn't be capable of a crime this terrible," she says. "Well, I'm over that now. Anybody is capable of anything, and in my world, there are no heroes. My trust is gone."

Joe agrees.

"This case changed how I view crime," he says. "This was my

first case with what I guess I would consider an 'innocent victim.' I hate to use that word, but it fits. Usually, there is a fine line between the victims from these suspects in cases. I mean cases where one druggie kills another. When a deal goes bad. But that's not what this case was. It was just totally out of character with what I had come to expect."

As for me, I guess I'm already hard. I admit to becoming cynical in my 42 years in Tyler, Texas, serving in law enforcement. Every time I think I've seen it all, something else pops up and I say, "Well, I didn't see that coming." But I have seen human weaknesses at all levels. It saddens me to say it, but I agree with Pam. I think every human being, logical, illogical, educated, uneducated, rich, poor, fat, tall, short, dark, ugly, whoever, whatever, is capable of anything.

I'll offer my final thoughts on the Marla Tabb murder. I don't have evidence to support my theories, at least no evidence beyond what I've shown you.

I believe that Michael Tabb was a deeply unhappy man; he had been so for years. I think his marriage to Marla Tabb produced a toxic union. Maybe, with different partners, they both would have turned out different – maybe even have been happy.

But their strengths didn't complement each other. Instead, their weaknesses fed off of each other. They fell into destructive, hurtful patterns of behavior. Was Michael a wimp? Was Marla a shrew? I don't know. I do believe that's what they thought of each other.

They both also fought dirty. Now, I know something about marriage (I'm on my third), and I know that people have to learn how to fight. You have to learn to guard your words. What you say, even in anger, can never be taken back.

From what we know now, it seems that Michael and Marla Tabb never held back. They unleashed their anger on each other, and it was Katy-bar-the-door.

Deep down, we know that Michael disappointed Marla. He wasn't the ambitious, charming, upwardly mobile preacher she had spent her youth dreaming of. The "glamour shots" she had taken to help advance her music career indicate she was plenty ambitious herself. Suffering through years as a Navy wife and then being given a small church in a smaller Texas town must have seemed like a cruel penance to her.

For his part, we know Michael felt humiliated by Marla. His career was repeatedly undermined by her actions. Even before they had arrived in Troup, she had alienated some key leaders in the church. By the time they moved in, a significant portion of the church was thinking hard about just telling the young family to "keep on moving."

I believe the alcohol abuse, the strip clubs, perhaps even the escorts (though we never proved there were any) were symptoms of a deeper problem – Michael Tabb was deeply unhappy and looking for anything that would salve those wounds.

Was he struggling, personally, with homosexuality? I don't know and I don't care. It's not needed to understand the why of this case. It's enough that he was miserable, so miserable that in a moment of extreme anger, he saw only one way out.

What happened on that hot Monday in August?

I believe that the arguing began early and lasted much of the day. Who knows what it was about; it probably had a lot to do with the church, the parsonage, and Marla's dissatisfaction. She probably took the opportunity to berate him about his drinking.

I believe – and this is just my gut feeling – that at some point, she used an unthinkable weapon. I believe she might – just might – have accused him of molesting their 2-year-old son in the bath. She had her suspicions. He dismissed those as ridiculous, but who is to say she wouldn't bring them back up in a moment of anger?

That kind of accusation is career-ending for a preacher. The charge doesn't even have to be proven. Just the accusation is enough to ruin everything Michael Tabb had worked for so long.

In my mind, that's the one thing that could have pushed Michael to the breaking point. As I have said before, I believe that in his anger, he turned to leave. He got as far as the carport, but with that loose table leg in hand, he turned back to express his rage.

Michael Tabb brings to my mind the Preacher, who wrote the book of Ecclesiastes. He sought spiritual stature and even worldly pleasures, but they proved of no help.

Then I looked on all the works that my hands had wrought, and on the labor that I had labored to do: and, behold, all was vanity and vexation of spirit, and there was no profit under the sun.

And I turned myself to behold wisdom, and madness, and folly: for what can the man do that cometh after the king? Even that which hath been already done.

Then I saw that wisdom excels folly, as far as light excels darkness...

Therefore I hated life; because the work that is wrought under the sun is grievous unto me: for all is vanity and vexation of spirit.

Michael Tabb despaired of life. Marla Tabb paid for that, with hers.

In Celebration of
The Life of
Marla McCown Tabb

April 25, 1967 – August 5, 2002

Funeral Service
WOODLAND BAPTIST CHURCH
August 9, 2002 10:00 AM
Officiating
Reverend Jim Sliger

Cover of Marla Tabb funeral program.

Pam and Joe

Smith County Sheriff's Office

Three amigos

Troup Police Department and 200 S. Virginia

SCSO

200 S. Virginia - Front view

200 S. Virginia - Back view

Marla McCown Tabb with baby

Personal photos collected as evidence by SCSO

297

Marla McCown Tabb with baby

Personal photos collected as evidence by SCSO

Turned over lamp at murder scene

SCSO

Truck bed with wipe marks

Truck at murder scene

SCSO crime scene photos

Telling evidence

Table at murder scene

SCSO crime scene photos

Tabb murder scene

Courtesy of Tyler Morning Telegraph

Time Out club

SCSO surveillance photo

Michael Tabb enters Smith County courthouse

Courtesy of Tyler Morning Telegraph

Judge Diane DeVasto, Tabb and attorney "Buck" Files

Courtesy of Tyler Morning Telegraph

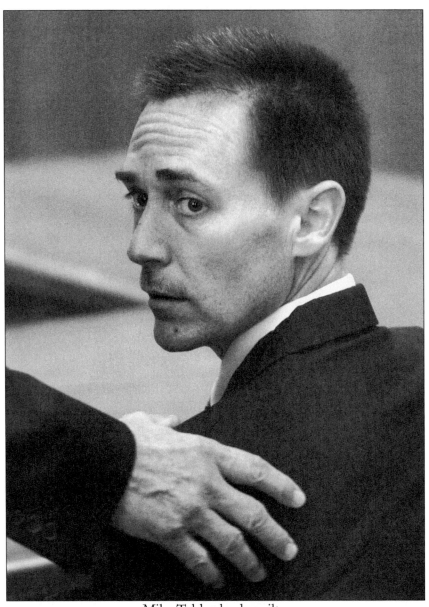

Mike Tabb pleads guilty

Courtesy of Tyler Morning Telegraph

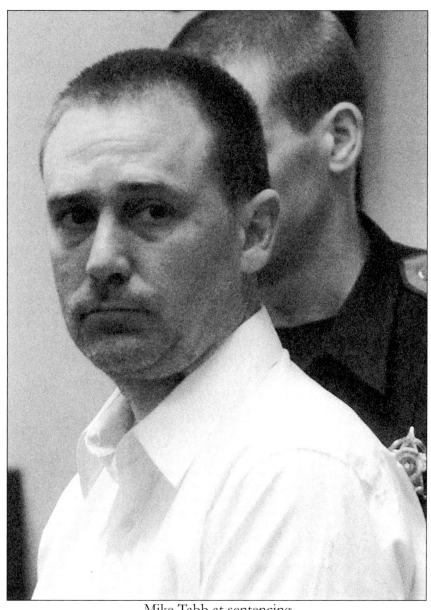

Mike Tabb at sentencing

Courtesy of Tyler Morning Telegraph

About the author:

Sheriff J.B. Smith was continuously elected sheriff of Smith County, Texas, from 1976, serving until his retirement at the end of 2012. He was one of the longest serving sheriffs in the state. He managed a department of 350 personnel and his staff oversaw as many as 1,000 jail inmates at a time. In his last five years in office, his staff booked in more than 66,000 prisoners.

Sheriff J.B. Smith

Sheriff Smith is a graduate of Tyler Junior College and the University of Texas at Tyler, with a bachelor of science degree in criminal justice. He is also a graduate of the national FBI Academy.

Throughout his tenure, his department was responsible for investigating many crimes, including murders. His investigators solved 80 percent of those cases, which is 20 percent above the national average.

In the late 1970s, Sheriff Smith brought in the University of Texas at Tyler to study the education level of most prisoners. They found that 75 to 80 percent of jail inmates did not have a high school education. This finding led him to contact the Texas Education Agency to help bring GED classes to the detention facilities. This is just one of the many programs he pioneered that has set a standard for other sheriffs to follow.

Sheriff Smith is one of the first sheriffs in East Texas to reintroduce the use of prisoner labor for the benefit of numerous non-profit organizations, such as the Junior League, the East Texas State Fair, the Salvation Army, Heart of Tyler-Main Street Program, the Historic Aviation Museum, the East Texas Crisis Center and others. Also, for many years, inmates have picked up an average of 55 tons of trash per year from Smith County roadways.

As a licensed Texas auctioneer, he holds numerous local auctions for various non-profit organizations. In addition, as a member of the National Speakers Association, Sheriff Smith has been called on to speak to different organizations throughout the nation.

His first book, "The Christmas Day Murders," was published in September 2006. This true crime book has been distributed to numerous criminal justice classes in colleges throughout Texas. Only one in 10 books published sells over 4,000 copies, and Sheriff Smith's book has exceeded expectations.

Sheriff Smith is proud of the many the qualified and experienced team of crime-scene investigators who not only worked these murders, but are called upon to direct or assist in operations all over the state.

On his ranch in the northeast part of Smith County, the sheriff has raised a small herd of longhorn cattle, horses, and emu named Big Bird, one flying squirrel, a fox family, and a major crop of ticks, red bugs, fire ants and armadillos.

His philosophy on life is "Blessed are those who laugh at themselves, for they will never cease to be amused.

Written on the side of the patrol cars, during Sheriff J.B. Smith's term in office, were the words "We Proudly Service." And he really meant it.

Photo by Randy Phillips Photography